HEALTHY ANGER MANAGEMENT

OVERCOME YOUR EMOTIONS AND CONQUER YOUR ANGER

HAYDEN HARPER

CONTENTS

INTRODUCTION

A moment of patience in a moment of anger prevents a thousand moments of regret.

— ALI IBN ABI TALIB

It's common to worry about living an unhappy life and the negative consequences of our actions. On occasion, we make decisions that seem small but significantly impact our happiness. Other times, we may feel like we cannot control ourselves, and a lack of self-control can be a big contributor to frustration and anger.

That's why one of the keys to a happy life is never to let your anger control you. In this sense, anger management is crucial in improving your overall well-being.

Anger is a primary emotion, as it has evolutionary value, is present early on in life, and has cross-cultural universality and differentiated autonomic patterns from other emotions.[1] Then, as a natural emotion, anger is something everyone experiences in response to something unjust, disappointing, stressful, or threatening. It has strong communication aspects for human beings, so it embraces a great constructive potential rather than destructive. This emotion says a lot about your personality and temperament, but most importantly, how balanced your life is.

Anger can be healthy and helpful when it motivates you to take action against injustice or unfairness. Even so, it's a serious mistake to consider anger as a totally adaptive and constructive mechanism and neglect its harmful and toxic aspects, such as the state of insecurity, carelessness, and defensiveness from which it emerges.

This emotion can be toxic and destructive when it becomes habitual and out of control. If you have a tendency to get angry quickly and easily, it will have a serious impact on your health, relationships, and quality of life. It can cause many problems.

Often, you might feel overwhelmed or stressed due to the angry atmosphere surrounding you at home or at work. It's possible that every little thing makes you constantly frustrated, so you find yourself having trouble controlling your emotions and feeling as if you're going to have an outburst. You might have engaged in arguments, screamed at people, or said harsh words to your loved ones because of your short temper.

Moreover, anger may cause inward aggression. In this case, you hurt yourself by, for example, thinking negatively, telling yourself discouraging words, denying basic needs like food, or avoiding any kind of social interaction and entertainment.

Frequent outbursts affect one's decisions, behavior, and relationships. Anger is often associated with interpersonal conflicts, erratic driving, negative evaluations by others, property destruction, inappropriate risk-taking, accidents, and substance abuse, among others. These anger outbursts make people around you feel upset and embarrassed, which can affect mental and physical health.

Fortunately, there are various strategies and exercises to manage anger more effectively. The best way to deal with anger is to understand how you respond to it. The concept of anger management is used to define the set of skills needed to recognize when you, or someone else, is becoming angry, and then take the appropriate actions to address the situation in a positive manner.

Anger is a very complex emotion; hence, anger management is not just about avoiding the feeling of anger, but also about understanding what triggers it and how you can control it in a healthier way so that it doesn't negatively affect yourself or others.

Positive emotions stand in stark contrast to negative emotions such as fear, shame, and anger, which narrow our attention and make us defensive, closed to curiosity, and less capable of creating alternative ways to be. While hurt (which fosters perspective-taking) needs full exploration, its impact on suppressing positive emotions is also worth exploring.

Truly making cultivating positive emotions a priority may provide a counterbalance to proneness to angry outbursts, as it enhances general emotional and physical well-being. Some potential benefits of anger management include healthier relationships, better judgment, reduced stress, and effective communication.

In this sense, a life free from anger will eventually increase self-satisfaction, helps build stronger coping skills and emotional resources, and promotes better health and longevity; this is because a happier mental state is linked to increased immunity. In general, positive feelings increase resilience, which at the same time helps manage stress and enables you to bounce back better when faced with setbacks.

Happiness embraces many shades, from peace and tranquility to joy and ecstasy, as it's the only human state that measures overall physical and mental well-being and results from harmony among our inner parts.[2] Happy people still feel anger, frustration, boredom, loneliness, and sadness from time to time. However, when faced with discomfort, they have a sense of optimism that things will get better, they can deal with what's happening, and can feel happy again.

WHY THIS BOOK?

If, during the past few months, you feel like your anger or bad temper has taken the best of you more than once, it's time to work on yourself. As we mentioned above, anger is one of the most common negative human emotions, but being angry all the time isn't healthy. An awareness and understanding of your anger can help you gain personal development in this area and change your life for the better.

Anger management is a great skill that can be learned, practiced, and improved at any time. During the process, you won't be alone. In this book, you'll find a comprehensive guide with the tools you need to manage stress and anger in different areas of your life. Whether at home, at work, or in your relationships, this book will teach you how to stay calm and in control by using practical and simple exercises.

You'll also learn to identify the different types of anger expressions, communicate better with others, keep your home a happy place, set boundaries, and resolve conflict in a healthy way. As a result, you'll become mentally healthier and begin to think of anger as a means to go through life positively.

When you can manage your anger effectively, you'll be more motivated to adopt assertive behaviors, increasing your life expectancy. The ultimate goal is then for you to live a long and happy life in which anger and other negative feelings do not control you.

ABOUT THE AUTHOR

Hi! I'm Hayden Harper. As an expert in anger issues and family relationships, I've seen firsthand the kind of environment that anger creates, so I know the importance of recognizing and avoiding the triggers that make people angry.

Unfortunately, no one is immune to the negative impacts of anger. A failure to recognize and understand your levels of anger causes several problems. It pulls you apart, triggers conflict, and hurts the relationships you need to function.

It impacts your ability to think clearly, patience, productivity, overall happiness, and even puts your health at risk. The average adult gets angry at least once a day, and gets annoyed or irritated two to three times a day.

Nowadays, the world is experiencing record levels of stress and anger. Millions of people suffer from chronic anger which poisons their lives daily. Although more and more people are becoming very aware of their anger, many others fail to recognize this emotion when it occurs.

This is why I want to help you manage your anger for your personal growth and that of your loved ones. My main goal is to guide you and present you with the tools to develop coping mechanisms for dealing with stress and anger while cultivating a more positive mindset and healthy lifestyle. However, it still remains your choice whether to keep your anger bottled up or to learn how to channel your anger constructively.

That said, are you ready to make a change and take your first steps towards a happier life?

1

THE ANGER ENCYCLOPEDIA

Anger is just anger. It isn't good. It isn't bad. It just is. What you do with it is what matters. It's like anything else. You can use it to build or to destroy. You just have to make the choice.

— JIM BUTCHER

WHAT IS ANGER?

Anger is an alerting phenomenon for you and others that provides a basis for communication. Psychologist Howard Kassinove defines anger as a negative emotional state associated with hostile thoughts, physiological arousal, and maladaptive behaviors.[1]

Anger is a "phenomenological feeling state" associated with specific cognitive and perceptual distortions and deficiencies (such as attributions of blame, injustice, preventability, and intentionality), subjective labeling, physiological changes, and action tendencies to engage in socially constructed and reinforced organized behavioral patterns.[2]

The word 'anger' is also an adjective that describes a tone of displeasure, madness, irritation, or antagonism toward someone or something. In some cases, anger becomes uncontrollable and destructive, resulting in violence or rage episodes.

Anger is reflected across distinct components: The arousal component, as in stress reactivity with concomitant autonomic arousal, and cognitive components, including heightened attention to threat, hyper-vigilance, and hostile attributions.[3] Moreover, it's classified according to the way it's expressed. Anger expressions can manifest through active or passive behaviors. The most common signs are classified as either verbal or nonverbal.

- **Verbal.** An angry person can employ verbal discharge and a whole series of specific communications to others to promote the removal of the threat. Others around this person are also alerted to their state of motor readiness, and if their verbal communications are clear enough, the message will help remove the threat. Verbal discharge serves to reduce muscle tension. An angry person expresses their emotions by raising their voice, yelling, arguing, cursing, and even expressing sarcasm. They might use insults or hurtful words if the anger is directed at another person.

- ***Nonverbal.*** When displayed nonverbally, anger will cause the body to experience physical changes. Anger will manifest through your body language. For example, the angry person experiences an involuntary increase in muscle tension almost simultaneously with a perception of threat or obstruction, and they are alerted to a strong need for motor discharge. This type of anger might go along with physical aggression, such as screaming, hitting things, slamming doors, or lashing out at another person. It usually aims to hurt those who triggered your anger, either emotionally or physically, but in some cases, it may lead back to yourself.

Each of these are not mutually exclusive; it is possible to see a person who expresses their anger in both of these two ways, even simultaneously.

ANGER AS AN EMOTION

In Dr. W. Doyle Gentry's words, emotion is a compound word: 'e' stands for 'energy' and 'motion' for 'movement.' Emotions encourage you to act in ways that protect you from threats, and lead to social attachments, engaging in enjoyable pursuits, reattachment after a significant loss, or encourage you to explore your environment.[4] Therefore, anger is a social emotion, always addressed towards someone or something (i.e., events, people, or even yourself).

Anger has some advantages as an emotion. First, it can be distracting when you experience pain or fear, and if you experience both at the same time, you can be preoccupied with concentrating on things other than yourself. Therefore, anger can temporarily protect you from dealing with your painful feelings.

Anger as a Substitute Emotion

Anger as a substitute emotion can be helpful in avoiding pain, which can be done consciously or unconsciously.

Anger as a Protective Emotion

Anger can act as a protective emotion that helps you recognize and deal with other negative feelings, hide the reality for a short time, and avoid feeling vulnerable or weak.

Anger as an Emotion of Righteousness

Anger can be an emotion of righteousness, power, and moral superiority. Under this emotion, you are angry with the cause.

THE TRIGGERS OF ANGER

A feeling encompasses a wide range of mental processes and individual experiences. Throughout evolution, anger has had an adaptive role in survival with its fundamental involvement in the fight-or-flight reaction to threat detection.[5]

A fight-or-flight response refers to an automatic physiological reaction to a situation perceived as stressful or frightening. Such perception activates your sympathetic nervous system and causes a stress response that prepares your body to fight or flee. Other emotions that cause this reaction include fear, excitement, and anxiety.

Anger and stress can feed on each other. When you're under too much pressure and, consequently, feeling overly stressed, you're more prone to anger, and in this state, both anger and stress can become more challenging to control. Factors contributing to stress, like threats to social standing, emotional well-being, or just too many demands, can also lead to anger. When physiologically aroused by the body's stress response, emotions can escalate more quickly, leading to quick temper management.[6]

Psychologist Jerry Deffenbacher says that high anger drivers have the following characteristics: They're highly judgmental of other people's driving, and second, they have contempt for how others drive.[7]

A trigger that can be either rational or irrational, external or internal, mainly causes anger. When you're in pain, emotionally hurt, threatened, or involved in a confrontation, anger can run out. Anger is then an intense emotion that makes you react to a threat—real or imagined—which can cause you to be aggressive, hostile, and even violent.

Therefore, provocation—a stimulus perceived as threatening—is a common activator of anger. This emotion also arises in response to other people's behaviors or words that you consider offensive or demeaning.

Psychologists also argue that sometimes people use anger to replace other emotions they don't want to deal with (i.e., emotional pain, grief, sadness, fear, loneliness, etc.). In this case, anger is a secondary emotion or side effect. Some common triggers are:

- being stressed or worried
- the loss of loved ones
- being fired or failing in a project
- stress due to financial problems or debt
- going through a breakup or divorce
- failing at doing something
- being fatigued (Feeling anger involves energy as it excites you, so your adrenaline flows, and after that, you feel exhausted.)
- rudeness and poor interpersonal skills
- hunger
- sexual frustration
- injustice (i.e., infidelity, bullying, humiliation, etc.)
- suffering a physical condition

- a symptom of a medical condition like depression, substance abuse, ADHD (attention-deficit/hyperactivity disorder), and bipolar disorder
- criminal activity committed against you or a loved one (i.e., theft, violence, sexual offenses, etc.)
- hormonal changes

In addition, anger mostly emerges under conditions of need, love, and involvement. While growing up, you feel anger more often towards your parents and relatives. In your later years, you feel frequent anger towards those you love, those you need, or situations you get involved in.

We'll dive deeper into the triggers of anger in Chapter 2.

THE SIGNS OF ANGER

Emotions like anger are more than a state of mind—they can trigger physical changes. When you're angry, your body experiences certain biological and physiological changes. Anger creates a surge of energy; chemicals such as adrenaline enter the bloodstream when this happens. As a result, your body presents some physical symptoms that affect your reasoning, and then your physical and mental health. Some of the physical signs of anger are listed below:

- increased energy levels
- rubbing the face
- tightness in the chest
- legs going weak
- increased muscle tension
- increased heart rate and respiration
- raised blood pressure
- spike in hormones like adrenaline, noradrenaline, and cortisol
- increased body temperature

Every person reacts in a different way. In some cases, you express your anger through:

- raised voices
- rapid heartbeats
- stomach ache
- feeling hot in the neck/face
- tightly clasping one hand with the other
- dizziness
- clenched fists
- frowning or scowling
- clenching the jaw or grinding your teeth
- trembling or shaking lips and hands

- sweating excessively
- hitting an object or even another person

Emotionally, you can feel:

- rudeness
- losing your sense of humor
- a desire to escape from the situation
- sad or depressed
- irritated
- humiliated
- guilty or resentful towards other people or situations
- a strong feeling or desire to lash out verbally or physically

Furthermore, anger can energize you to retaliate. Studies indicate that about 25% of anger incidents involve thoughts of revenge[8] and expressions used to reflect the subjective experience such as feelings of being mad and enraged, among many others.

Anger vs Aggression

Based on what we've discussed so far, anger is a primary and intuitive emotion that can show up from time to time. In fact, you're more likely to feel irritated if your basic human needs (such as food, shelter, sex, sleep, etc.) are not met or jeopardized somehow. It's hidden or unexpressed anger that's likely to cause arguments, physical fights, physical abuse, assault, and self-harm.

Anger is a manifestation of the broader phenomenon of aggression. "'To be angry' is considered to be an aggressive act, and 'to feel angry' is considered the subjective awareness of aggressive impulses".[9] Aggression is an intentional behavior aiming to harm another person, being a response to frustration, pain, or threats. Therefore, it's not inborn but learned during human development.

Aggression includes violence, hostility, hatred, and all manifestations of destructiveness and often reflects a desire for dominance and control. In this case, an aggressive person's behaviors may include shoving, beating others, or hitting objects, and can escalate to bullying, marital violence, child and elder abuse, or gang and criminal activities.

Though some people may act aggressively when angry, anger doesn't automatically generate physical aggression or violent behavior, as it's often a choice. We can separate anger from attack. Research shows that 90% of aggressive incidents are preceded by anger; however, only 10% of anger experiences are followed by aggression.[10]

Anger vs Hostility

Like anger, hostility is a behavioral manifestation. Anger is often linked to hostility, as the two phenomena may occur simultaneously. However, their main difference is that hostility, hate, and violence always have a destructive component, whereas anger does not.

For instance, "feeling hostile" always involves the wish or intent to inflict harm or pain on another person or object, and "being hostile" always involves inflicting or trying to inflict some destruction (psychological or physical) upon another. Consequently, hostility doesn't allow the feeling to play its role by removing the threats or obstructions; Instead, it tends to destroy this primary function itself.

Anger vs Violence

Violence can occur in conjunction with anger, and that actual destruction is often associated with the angry state. Violence happens when anger cannot serve as an excellent alerting process for the angry person themselves or for other people who can remove the threat, mainly because of poor interpersonal communication.

Violence also occurs when anger is unexpressed. The threats that caused it cannot be removed, and the presence of the threat continues in memory. Subsequent threats and the automatic responses to them are destructive.

All of us can remember experiences of threat, anxiety, and anger, and these memories influence the perception of danger throughout life. There are signs of anger and anxiety concerning particular situations and people. Such signs are constant and predictable, and consist of structural personality features that are likely to instigate violence. Because these special structural features are necessary to account for anger, this is both qualitatively and quantitatively different from violence.

In addition, violence occurs when there is too much anxiety associated with the angry state itself, no matter the experience with particular threats. This may be because of the intensity of the perceived threat and excessive guilt about the experience of feeling angry, or extreme fear of destructive thoughts or words.

Anger vs Fear

Like fear, anger is the result of a psychological interpretation of aroused feelings under certain circumstances. Both share a great number of common characteristics, and one of them is that they're characterized by similar central nervous system arousal. Second, both cause the same physiological symptoms: a sinking feeling in your stomach, sweating, trembling, and an increased heart rate.

However, the physical manifestations of anger and fear are different. Heart rate increases during both emotional episodes, but skin temperature and electrical conductance do not do the same: When you're angry, they increase, and when you're scared, they decrease. Likewise, both have opposite outcomes on the perception of risk. Fearful people express pessimistic risk estimates and risk-averse choices, whereas angry people express optimistic risk estimates and risk-seeking options.[11]

Finally, anger increases approach motivation, whereas fear induces avoidance.[12] You need to understand their differences, as it will help you take the proper steps to control them.

Anger vs Depression

Anger and depression have some aspects in common. Both are initiated in the brain and cause a chemical imbalance that makes individuals either repress or release their emotions. Likewise, they involve stress and frustration.

PRONENESS TO ANGER

People can interpret situations differently, but this doesn't mean that you'll interpret things 'wrong' if you're angry. How you respond to a situation depends on several factors in your life. For instance, your childhood and upbringing, past experiences, lifestyle, habits, and current circumstances (job, studies, romantic relationship, etc.).

This is the reason why some people are more prone to anger than others. Proneness to anger is examined concerning thoughts, physiological reactions, and physical activity. These physiological reactions are rapid responses to aversive stimuli. This refers to those who rapidly become angered by bad smells, heat, traffic jams, and annoying noises. Other people are slow to react, and seem not as bothered by such events. Genetic variability plays a big part in this case.[13]

On the other hand, some people learn physical expressions of anger by the forces of reinforcement and copying others. Evidence indicates that violent video games or listening to music with violent lyrics may fuel negative feelings in some people. These people learn to be hyper-alert and respond impulsively.[14]

Moreover, children, for example, can copy the behavior of anger from the adults around them who influence them by being hostile and making threats.[15] If those children grow up in a conflictive and hostile environment, they learn to berate and belittle themselves and then repeat this behavior when they're adults. This is why someone who has learned to act in an angry way may not realize that they have anger problems.

In addition, those who have been victims of abuse or bullying may develop anger problems due to the revenge principle. Bullying is a series of aggressive behaviors repeated intentionally to hurt others physically or emotionally. In the case of children, when being bullied by their peers, they tend to be more aggressive in turn, as they think such actions can protect them and make them more powerful or popular in their environment. Under these circumstances, their desire for revenge grows, leading to intense anger episodes. Eventually, the victim may become the bully.

An abused child or teenager can become hostile at some point towards others. In this sense, they engage in aggressive actions more and more, since they find that it helps raise their social status and position.

Adults can also be victims of bullying which can take place at home or in the workplace. People with anger problems usually target their family, friends, and co-workers. They take out their anger on others so that the latter feel the same humiliation and pain.

Research also suggests that the tendency to become angry is linked to high neuroticism and low agreeableness,[16] alongside other factors, such as:

- a fragile ego
- entitlement (considering that someone's rights and privileges are superior to others' privileges)
- attention to things that we cannot control
- concentration on external factors (believing well-being is influenced by external sources)
- external regulation of our emotions (for example, trying to regulate our feelings by controlling our environment)
- refusal to see other perspectives (different perspectives are perceived as threats)
- low tolerance for discomfort and ambiguity
- overfocus on blaming others

The next chapter will introduce the tools necessary to identify when your anger becomes a problem, so we'll dive deeper into what kind of triggers may cause it.

2

IDENTIFYING YOUR ANGER

You don't have to chase anger out of you. You allow it to be in you, embrace it tenderly, and then anger will subside and overcome the danger. During the practice, you have helped anger, and it will be transformed slowly. This practice enables you to acknowledge your anger with a smile.

— THICH NHAT HANH

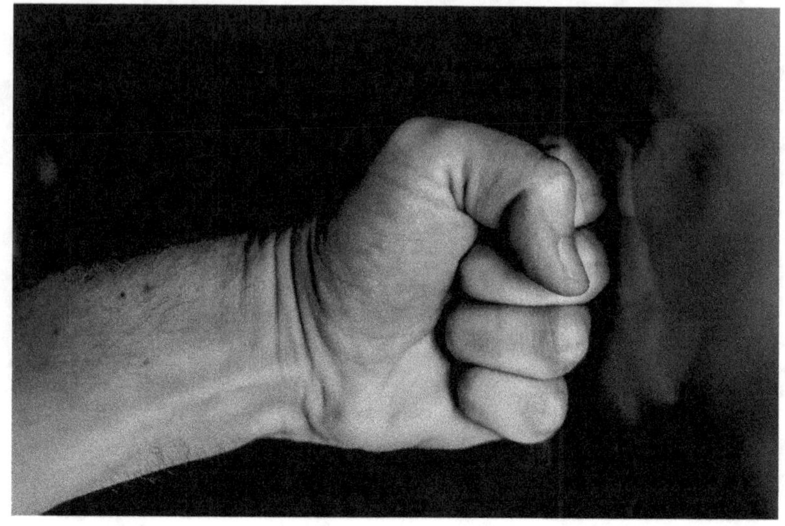

UNDERSTANDING YOUR ANGER

Adam is a seven-year-old child who was going through some significant issues at home related to a family breakdown. He was displaying a considerable temper by ignoring his teacher and kicking furniture and walls, shouting, and walking or running away when he was outraged.

Conversations with his parents, professors, and school counselor, alongside direct observations, led to identifying the following triggers of his anger:

- When people don't let him play with them.
- When they say he isn't good at football because he can't kick properly.

- When some children say nasty, hurtful things to him.
- When he fails to do something.

Adam thinks that people are like this because "they hate him." "They don't care how people feel sometimes. They think it's funny." He's able to recognize that this behavior is not correct and that those people are trying to have power over him.

During his anger episodes, Adam displays these traits:

- tightens his fists
- frowns
- quickened breathing and heart rate
- tense shoulders and face
- dizzy feeling
- shouts and yells
- hits objects
- experiences a "hot feeling"

Other observations and consultations with parents and teachers showed that the following deficits were affecting Adam's ability to cope in the previous situation:

- He cannot label his emotions.
- He is unable to ask for help in the classroom.

- He had no adaptive strategies in his repertoire for coping when somebody rejected or criticized him.
- He didn't know the consequences of his actions for himself or others.

After analyzing the previous aspects, it was possible to help him design anger management strategies based on understanding two key issues: First, knowing what sorts of things (and situations) he gets angry about. Second, he doesn't have to stay angry; there are techniques he can apply to feel better and improve the situation when that strong feeling runs out.

Here's Adam's plan for when he feels angry:

1. Count down from 10 with closed eyes. If this is embarrassing and people are looking, count quietly inside your head.
2. Breathe calmly. Count to two slowly in your head while breathing in, then breathe out slowly for another count of two.

Adam realized that he could relax his face and shoulders with this simple technique. He could also distinguish between deep breaths and calm breaths.

The key theme in Adam's plan was the self-belief that "I can learn to control myself. This is my plan. I am learning to do things that can help me make things better (not worse) when I have angry feelings." That belief was supported by his teacher's modeling, encouragement, and assurance.

In Adam's case, you can see how identifying your anger pattern is the key to successful anger management. If you can find the reason behind your anger, you can respond more appropriately and use that anger to your advantage.

WHY IS IT IMPORTANT TO IDENTIFY YOUR ANGER?

If you're like most people, you probably don't think about your anger very often. You might not even realize that you experience angry feelings constantly. But try as you might suppress it, your anger is a natural and universal response to the stressors of daily life.

When you repress anger, you build up pressure inside of you until it eventually comes out in the form of passive aggression or explosive rage. However, when you acknowledge and identify it, you can take control of those emotions rather than letting them control you.

Each of us experiences and handles anger differently. Some individuals become angry very quickly, while some rarely display anger. Sometimes, anger can suddenly appear and surprise everyone with its sudden onset and intensity. Angry feelings can be present for no apparent reason, and they can mask or replace other complicated emotions such as fear, hurt, guilt, jealousy, frustration, or shame.

Although anger is a complex emotion, learning how to identify and manage it is an ability that can be learned and perfected throughout the years. Learning to identify and manage your anger allows you to use it to improve your relationships, health, and quality of life.

JUSTIFIED VS UNJUSTIFIED ANGER

Anger can be helpful when justified, but not when it's unjustified. Justified anger can be used as a signal to take action to improve your situation or protect yourself from aggression or dangerous events. The social judgment of anger causes serious consequences to the angry individual. You may feel justified in committing an angry action, but if others don't see it that way, you can be in trouble.

Unjustified anger can lead to poor decision-making and harm your relationships, creating a dangerous situation. In extreme, uncontrolled anger can lead to violence and seriously damage young lives. It can cause the same adverse health outcomes as alcohol and drug abuse, as it prevents you from logical and rational thinking. For example, if a person uses anger to manipulate or control others and has people fear them, they become the abuser or the bully. Therefore, it's important to reduce the impact of unjustified anger by recognizing when it occurs.

Whether justified or unjustified, very often a seductive feeling of righteousness linked to anger offers a powerful but temporary boost to self-esteem. Sometimes we may feel a 'satisfying' sensation when angry, which is dangerous as we don't want to face the painful emotions of vulnerability. So, be careful not to take the easiest path.

Similarly, some people develop the unconscious habit of transforming their fears and vulnerability into anger to avoid dealing with it. It shows that you can use anger to transform vulnerability, helplessness, and fear into self-control, courage, and power. However, as I mentioned above, it becomes a problem when anger diverts your attention, making you forget that you're afraid and vulnerable.

THE ORIGINS OF ANGER

Anger doesn't always arise at the appropriate moment, and it sometimes overwhelms you, making you turn towards and lash out at things you perceive to be threatening, even if they aren't. Your anger can have its origins for many reasons.

Psychologists identified four ways of thinking associated with the internal sources of anger. The first is *emotional reasoning*. Those who reason emotionally often misinterpret everyday events and things others say as a direct threat or attack against them. Under this anger-causing type, individuals often become irritated at innocent things someone may tell them.

Second, *low tolerance for frustration and disappointment*. Anxiety and stress lower tolerance for frustration, which then causes you to see ordinary things as a threat.

Third, *unreasonable expectations*. You may have found yourself making demands without knowing the reality of the situation. If you can't have the things you expected or the situation doesn't go in a certain way, it lowers your tolerance for frustration and makes you angry.

Fourth, *rating people*. It triggers derogatory labeling of other people. This type of thinking dehumanizes others and makes it easier for you to be mad at them.

Moreover, according to the cognitive behavior theory, anger is attributed to several factors, such as past experiences, behavior learned from others, genetic predispositions, and lack of problem-solving ability.[1] Let's discuss some of them.

Reason #1: You Feel a Sense of Danger

We already discussed that anger is an emotional response linked to the fight-or-flight response. The emotions associated with this response are fear (which tends to keep us away from any threat), anxiety (which makes us anticipate events or situations that could wrong us), and anger.

Consequently, you can respond to the situation that causes anger when you feel endangered. Under a dangerous situation (theft, violence, death threat, etc.), irritation appears as energy to help you turn and face a threat and fight for your life.

Reason #2: You Are Facing Injustice

You might have experienced a rush of adrenaline or an urge to turn and fight against a specific situation that you consider unacceptable, for example, bullying, racism, or social injustice. This anger expression is very helpful, because it makes you channel your efforts toward promoting a change in society.

The level of anger under these circumstances will depend on how personally challenging or threatening you consider the injustice and how you usually feel and respond to anger. For some people, their fight response will be insignificant, so they'll just feel annoyed and have the need to act upon the situation. For others, that response will be stronger; the energy of anger will surge throughout their body, and they may shout or engage in a fight before they realize they're angry.

Reason #3: You Feel Rejected or Vulnerable

Threats to the self-concept or identity are among the principal triggers of anger.[2] Vulnerability, rejection, and sadness are all common reasons for anger. Rejection can be physically painful, and not all of us have been taught or developed coping skills to face such pain. What's more, many of us have been taught to be consistently strong, even in the most challenging situations, as being vulnerable can make us weak. As a result, any feeling of vulnerability, rejection, or sadness may lead our brains to think we're in danger, and eventually, anger springs up in our defense.

If you feel anger in these circumstances, it can cause you some issues, such as distracting you from the actual emotional response and situation that created the anger, meaning you don't attend to your actual emotional needs. Likewise, if you act on the rage and argue with the person who made you feel sad or rejected, they'll withdraw or fight back, the opposite of what you may want and need when you feel rejected, vulnerable, and sad.

Reason #4: You Are Affected by Outside Influence

Several external sources can cause you to get angry. For instance, people who attack others, people who criticize others' ideas and opinions, the lack of empathy in society, and people who are suffering from hunger, poverty, or crime, among others. In this case, an individual's level of tolerance for frustration is low due to environmental factors in their lives.

Reason #5: You Have Traumatic Memories

Anger issues can also be caused by traumatic or enraging events in one's life that have shaped one's personality. For instance, the death of someone you love, an accident, domestic violence, or illness, among others.

THE MYTHS OF ANGER

Before you learn how to manage your anger, you need to know what anger is and isn't. I want you to break down some of the myths linked to this emotion.

Myth #1: Anger Is a Negative Emotion

Not necessarily. Anger can only be harmful when out of control and is not used appropriately. Many positive benefits come with using anger appropriately, including coping with anxiety, depression, and stress. This emotion boosts your energy, enhances your communication and social skills, increases your self-esteem, and protects you against fear, pain (emotional and physical), and insecurity.

Myth #2: Anger Is a Positive Emotion

It's not good when anger leads to domestic violence, property damage, sexual abuse, drug addiction, ulcers, and self-mutilation. The intensity of your anger could range from deep annoyance to extreme rage. It's healthy to experience anger in response to specific situations from time to time. Still, sometimes people experience a huge wave of uncontrollable anger, which can escalate even when the provocation is insignificant. In this context, anger isn't a normal and natural emotion, but a great problem.

Myth #3: Anger Always Escalates Into Violence

This is false. There are many ways to use anger without hurting anyone, such as verbal expressions, passive-aggressiveness, non-cooperation, physical changes, and loneliness, among many others.

Myth #4: You Cannot Control How You Feel

This is partially true. You can't completely control how you feel, but you can reduce the intensity and frequency of your anger and choose your behavior. You need to accept your anger, but most importantly, you need to avoid those negative behaviors that uncontrolled anger wants you to perform.

Recognizing and accepting your emotions have positive outcomes; for example, both of these help you address those emotions (not stop feeling them) and demolish the unconscious beliefs. Similarly, changing your behavior significantly impacts your life as it makes it easier to improve your relationship with yourself and others.

Myth #5: Anger Management Will Never Work

Anger management helps you detect anger on time, see it coming, and handle it in a way that can lead to more productive results. When you can't control your anger, your emotions can run away from you. Using unhealthy expressions of your anger causes many inconveniences, including relationship, career, and legal problems. Even through therapeutic sessions and classes, anger management is beneficial in understanding your anger and learning to manage it better.

Myth #6: You Should Repress Your Anger

Anger management doesn't mean repressing or suppressing your emotions; sometimes this can be unhealthy. Anger can be used as a positive emotion if you learn to express it appropriately.

Suppressing your anger or never getting angry is just as unhealthy as extreme and violent expressions of anger. When we repress our feelings, it adds an unknown and risky element to them. Once those feelings find their way out, they can come in the form of an explosion instead of a natural expression.

Myth #7: The Older the More Irritable

As individuals get older, they report fewer negative emotions and greater emotional control. In fact, most of us tend to improve with age.

Myth #8: Anger Is All in the Mind

This is false. Emotions are primarily physical; if anger were only a state of mind, it wouldn't produce physical signs. We discussed in the previous chapter that anger starts to manifest in the muscles, and then goes throughout your whole body long before you notice what's happening.

Myth #9: Anger Is About Getting Revenge

One of the most common reasons behind anger is the strong desire to reinforce one's authority and independence—or improve one's image—but that doesn't mean that revenge or the intention to cause harm is implicit. Revenge is often a secondary trigger, and a third motive involves letting off steam over accumulated frustrations without intending to harm anyone else.

Myth #10: Only Certain Types of People Have a Problem With Anger

Anger is a universal emotion, no matter the gender, upbringing, or personality type.

Myth #11: Anger Results From Human Conflict

Sometimes anger comes from conflict. Most authors that have studied anger say that one can also get angry when they feel hunger, smell foul odors, have aches and pains, feel hot or cold, or are stuck in traffic jams or noisy places—none of which involve other people's actions.

Myth #12: Anger Makes Pain Disappear

Anger only distracts you from your pain. In general, anger doesn't solve the problems that made you feel vulnerable or fearful initially, but can create new issues, including social and health problems.

HOW CAN ANGER BE USEFUL?

All emotions have a purpose, and anger isn't the exception. It provides you with physical energy, and drives you to avoid the things in life that could threaten you and turn towards the things that could help you thrive.

Therefore, anger can be used as a signal to get your attention and motivate you to take action. It can be a signal to:

- *Express negative feelings*. When you feel angry, you might want to say or do things you'll regret later on. Ignoring angry feelings doesn't help anything and can lead to feelings of bitterness, resentment, or even hatred.
- *Express your needs*. When feeling angry, you might want to tell someone how they have hurt or inconvenienced you. This can be an opportunity to get what you need.
- *Set limits*. When someone does something you don't like or threatens you, anger can be a signal to set a limit. You can tell the person what you don't like and what you want. Ask for what you need. When someone's hurting or inconveniencing you, you might feel angry. You can ask this person to stop doing what they're doing and explain to them what you need.

HOW TO IDENTIFY YOUR ANGER

Anger often occurs when you face a painful experience alongside pessimistic thoughts, such as assumptions, personal assessments, or interpretations of situations that make you think something or someone can somehow hurt you.

You should identify what kind of events you often experience and which of them causes you the most anger. Knowing your anger triggers is essential, since you'll respond more effectively to anger when prepared for it. When you can anticipate the possibility of an angry outburst, you'll be able to express it constructively.

Unfair Treatment

We've all witnessed unfairness, and have all been victims of unfair treatment at school, home, or the office that make us feel mad, annoyed, or enraged.

Stress and Frustrations

Today, we're forced to deal with many things simultaneously, and face being under pressure constantly. Home, job, studies, and economic and social issues, among other factors, challenge us daily. When our stress levels increase, it can decrease our tolerance for frustration.

Disappointment

Who doesn't feel upset or angry when someone breaks a promise or lies to us? All of us do. We often face such situations with our partners, bosses, children, colleagues, or friends. An outburst of anger towards your employer or co-workers can get you fired at work.

For example, during my studies at university, working in big groups was very challenging for me. Being a perfectionist and a disciplined person, I just wanted team members to follow my way of working, and those who didn't have the same interest and passion as I did made me feel disappointed, frustrated, and angry. Once I recognized the source of my anger, I could find solutions to handle it and improve my relationship with my classmates.

Low Self-Esteem

No one likes to be criticized. Most people react to self-esteem threats with sadness, while some respond with anger. Self-esteem threats can be realistic or unfair. For example, receiving negative comments from your boss or professor, getting insulted or rejected by others, making a mistake in front of many people, bullying, losing a competition, or being a victim of discrimination.

Prejudice or Discrimination

Most people who face discrimination feel vulnerable, so they respond with irritation, anger, rage, or even violence. The most common themes of unfair treatment are racial differences, religious beliefs, sexual orientation, classism, disability, and appearance.

Getting Attacked

Unfortunately, the world is becoming more violent. The majority of people have been victims of some kind of violence or abuse, which can naturally cause anger, anxiety, or depression. Chronic abuse can take many forms, and ranges from subtle to blatant. This can be through domestic violence, assault, sexual abuse, war trauma, or verbal intimidation.

On the other hand, specific signs can indicate whether or not your anger is unhealthy and harmful:

- You're constantly impatient, hostile, and irritated.
- You always focus on negative experiences.
- You lose your temper quickly, even because of minor issues such as traffic, hunger, being late, hot weather, extra work, or headache.
- You feel you have to hide or repress your anger.
- You cannot control your anger.
- You often find yourself arguing with your loved ones or co-workers and getting angrier.
- Your anger is affecting your relationships and social life.
- You're getting physically violent when angry, or have the impulse to do violent things.
- You're anxious or depressed about your angry outbursts.

The next chapter will provide you with more information about the science of anger and how it alters your brain.

3

THE RIGHTS AND WRONGS OF ANGER

Use your anger for good. Anger to people is like gas to the automobile, it fuels you to move forward and get to a better place. Without it, we would not be motivated to rise to a challenge. It is an energy that compels us to define what is just and unjust.

— ARUN GANDHI

THE BRAIN AND ANGER

Located in the cerebral cortex are lobes and our thinking parts, where judgment and logic reside. The brain's control center is composed of the hypothalamus, amygdala, hippocampus, and limbic cortex. While each of these parts is located in different areas of the brain, they all work together in a specific order to help us perceive, process, regulate, and respond to emotions.

When it comes to feelings and emotions, there are regions in the brain, like the limbic system, associated with only six major emotions (fear, anger, sadness, disgust, joy, and surprise). The limbic system is the emotional center of your brain. This four-level system is responsible for the regulation of emotions and memories, including motor functions.

Nevertheless, although a large portion of the brain is involved in regulating emotions in one way or another, the core process relies on communications between areas of the prefrontal cortex, particularly the medial regions and subcortical systems, including the amygdala, hippocampus, and basal ganglia.

The prefrontal cortex is akin to the control center, helping guide your actions, and thus also involved in emotional regulation. Cognitive control networks recruit the anterior cingulate cortex circuitry, as well as the dorsolateral prefrontal cortex, which is dedicated to cold, non-emotional, rational thinking.

The human brain then scans anything threatening; it processes all emotional stress guiding the body to respond. Humans' response to angry feelings depend on how balanced the communication is between several brain regions. When this connection is disrupted, it makes you react aggressively.

The brain's frontal regions inhibit your automatic response to sadness, frustration, and anger. Research shows that uncontrolled anger affects the neurons in the hypothalamus—the brain's command center that regulates stress responses.

Anger causes neurotransmitter chemicals in the brain, catecholamines, to flow throughout the body, boosting energy levels for some minutes. Then, such an energy boost causes a chain reaction in other parts of your body: Your heart rate and blood pressure increase, and your breathing intensifies.

The Part of the Brain That Controls Anger

Now, where does anger come from? Scientists identified a particular area in the brain—called the amygdala—that processes anger and fear, and motivates us to take action. This area is linked to emotional responses towards any threat experienced. Henceforth, anger begins within the two almond-shaped structures.

The amygdala is found within the limbic system, a storage facility responsible for emotional memories and behavioral responses. It's the brain's primary controlling nerve nucleus for emotions and feelings, formed by numerous nerves connected to different parts of the brain, like the neocortex and the visual cortex. Anger begins with the amygdala, which stimulates the hypothalamus to initiate the fight-or-flight response.

The hypothalamus is the gland that controls emotional responses and hormone release, as well as regulates body temperature. In this process, the gland releases hormones like adrenaline and cortisol that activate a physical and emotional alarm in your mind. As these hormones enter the bloodstream, you notice some of the physical changes described in the previous chapters.

With such a boost of energy that follows this process, your body prepares to act. The impact of the hormonal flushing continues for some minutes, during which a person who experiences anger often loses control and says or does things they will later regret when the thinking part of the brain comes back to normality and recovers its function.

An increased propensity for anger has also been positively associated with increased volume in the amygdala. Consequently, people who suffer from damage in this area of the brain may have trouble controlling their emotions, especially anger and aggression.[1] Similarly, most scientists agree that hostile and aggressive behavior is linked to a hyperactive response in the amygdala, reducing the activity in the brain's prefrontal cortex.[2]

The amygdala then helps to coordinate responses to things in the environment, particularly things which provoke an emotional response. It's responsible for determining which memories are stored, and where they'll be stored in your brain. If the information is considered threatening, the amygdala sends a distress signal to the brain. Your brain then produces a series of physiological reactions from rapid heartbeats, high blood pressure, tight muscles, and the release of adrenaline.

In other words, the information that comes from external stimuli is perceived by the amygdala, where a decision is made about whether the information is sent to the limbic area of the brain or to the cortex. When trying to assess if the situation is dangerous, the amygdala compares the situation with a series of memories from your past experiences.

Parts of the prefrontal cortex in the brain can also help regulate an angry reaction. The amygdala (as the emotional center) may sense a significant event that's frightening, and it'll relay this information to the prefrontal cortex (as the controlling center). The transition from anger to rage is interrupted before the individual gets out of control.

As explained above, the amygdala is a key indicator of threats in your brain. Its main function is to assess and process the emotional and social aspects of your behavior; thus, it makes your brain react to the threatening stimuli before the prefrontal cortex, responsible for the brain's judgments and controlling aggressive impulses, evaluates the consequences.

To summarize, numerous brain regions work together to process and respond to emotional situations. When it comes to emotions, it turns out there are regions of the brain, particularly the limbic system. The more primal emotions—those that affect things like breath and heartbeat—are all controlled by the amygdala.

When the amygdala activates anger, the prefrontal cortex stimulates the aggressive behavior derived from that anger. The amygdala is so effective at alerting us to threats that it gets us to react before the cortex, in charge of thinking and judgments, verifies that our reactions are justified.

On the other hand, hormones such as serotonin have an impact on regulating anger and aggression. In fact, serotonin deficiency appears to be related to pathological, violent forms of aggressiveness; hence, people experiencing aggressive behavior maintain lower levels of serotonin compared to those with non-aggressive behavior.[3]

How Anger Changes Your Way of Thinking

The two ways in which people express their anger are not mutually exclusive, and it's possible to encounter an individual who expresses their anger in both of these ways. In these circumstances, anger may play a role in merely emphasizing one's irritation, and can contribute to resolving a problem. In such cases, it's difficult to contain your emotions, so you may behave in ways that you otherwise wouldn't.

When you've identified the pattern of thinking that's driving your anger, you can learn to adjust the way you think about everything. The change from a primal emotion like fear, sadness, or loss happens quickly, which is why deliberate thinking is necessary to determine what lies beneath your anger.

Studies show that anger can change your perception of risk, making you more impulsive or underestimating the potential bad outcomes.[4] In this sense, anger can make you brave. Anger also reframes the manner you interact with others. Under this feeling, you tend to think more negatively, perceiving others as a threat and blaming them for your situation and way of response. This issue may create a vicious circle in which you feel angrier with the offending people.

GENDER IMPLICATIONS WITH ANGER

According to several studies, both men and women tend to feel angry at the same frequency and intensity.

Researchers found that gender socialization may influence the way that men and women deal with anger.

Both men and women are frequently shamed about their anger, though they seem to be experiencing anger in different ways. The key difference commonly identified was that men felt less effective when forced to curb their anger, whereas women seemed to have a better ability to curb their impulsive, immediate reactions to anger.

Studies found that, on average, men are more likely to be more aggressive than women, as they're less effective in containing their anger. In general, no one is comfortable dealing with anger, but men consider it acceptable to display it under certain circumstances, such as competitiveness and combativeness.[5]

From a young age, boys are traditionally taught that emotions such as sadness or fear aren't acceptable. As a result, in adulthood they tend to hide their shame or pain, and that's when anger enters the scene. Scientists have concluded that men will often display anger when they're experiencing fear, frustration, or depression.[6]

Compared to men, women seem to control their impulses to anger better.[7] One study conducted at the University of Pennsylvania School of Medicine found that while the amygdala is a similar size in men and women, the orbital frontal cortex is much larger in women.[8]

These findings indicate that there are distinct patterns in the experiences and expressions of anger, that the patterns are significantly related to gender roles, and that these patterns are differentially associated with problems or risks for mental health. Nevertheless, researchers continue to discover differences between the way men and women experience anger to remove stereotypes about gender and patterns of anger.

THE GOOD SIDE OF ANGER

You hear people talk about using anger as a motivating force at times, turning anger into positive energy. Instead of engaging in destructive behaviors when you're feeling angry, try to direct your anger towards positive actions.

Many of the longer-term effects of anger are negative, but it has survival value and some positives due to its alerting function. Despite the provocation and situational triggers, well-managed anger is couched in distinct internal states that can escalate in a positive feedback loop.

Anger as a powerful emotion can make you feel better under the right circumstances, proving helpful to express negative feelings. It can provide you with a rest from feelings of vulnerability, helping you release tensions or any frustrations. For those who are long-suffering victims of domestic abuse, and whose anger reaches the boiling point so that it encourages them to leave their abusive relationship, anger is a positive force in their lives.

Likewise, anger is highly related to love, first due to its connection to need and involvement, and second due to its constructive communication factors. When clear communication accompanies it, it's a sign of basic respect for the person you love.

Besides, anger is a strong motivator for achieving personal goals, protecting yourself from dangerous situations, and finding solutions to problems. Sometimes anger is an appropriate response to injustice as well, encouraging you to right the wrongs you see in society, such as racism and violence.

Expanding on the above, let's discuss in detail the main reasons why anger can be a positive emotion.

Reason #1: It Gives You Some Energy

As we've explained in the previous sections, when you experience anger, your body receives a rush of cortisol that makes you more energetic. Thus, it's stimulating and gives you the strength to overcome difficulties. Since anger tends to strike when you feel threatened or challenged, it gives you the power to stand up for yourself and speak your mind.

Reason #2: It's a Motivator

Anger serves as a positive and creative force to motivate you to find solutions to problems and stand up for yourself. Frequently, you might encounter obstacles that need to be removed or situations that require special attention. Anger then prepares you to deal with them so that you can move further.

Although anger leads to more creative ideas, it's only in small doses, so this creative advantage of an angry mood doesn't last for long.[9]

Reason #3: It Promotes Survival

Anger is part of our primitive instincts that help us protect ourselves against dangerous events or aggression. Anger helps you to be vigilant about fears and threats and automatically pushes you to fight back against them and act as quickly as possible.

Reason #4: It Makes You Aware of Injustice

Unjust situations like disrespect or violence can trigger your anger. This is because anger works as an internal guidance system that indicates when something isn't right or is out of place and you should do something about it. This response can prevent people from taking advantage of others.

Reason #5: It Can Be Calming

Feeling angry implies physical and emotional pain or distress. When this happens, anger helps you discharge the tension in your body once you take action about the situation, which eventually calms your nerves. This is the reason why after an angry reaction, you may feel calm.

Reason #6: It Gives You Some Self-Control

Anger is linked to a deep need for control, since its protective component helps you feel in charge rather than helpless. When displaying your anger appropriately, you're better positioned to fulfill your needs and control everything in your life. Therefore, it's important not to become obsessed with the sense of power anger gives you.

There's evidence that anger can make you more rational and analytical. Scientists have studied how anger influences thinking and decision-making, and have discovered that anger-induced action can come from "clear-minded and deliberative processing".[10]

Reason #7: It Covers Your Pain

Anger can be considered a defense mechanism that prevents you from feeling more painful emotions. The emotion may distract you from your pain and other threatening feelings. For instance, when someone you love dies, you may use anger to block or limit the pain and sadness from your loss, which is more difficult to bear than your anger.

Reason #8: It Protects Your Values and Beliefs

Anger is also a social and personal value indicator and regulator that makes you aware of your beliefs and what you stand for. This is activated when your values aren't in harmony with the situation you're facing, which motivates you to rectify the discrepancy and take action to change the situation according to your values.

Reason #9: It Pushes You Towards Your Goals

Being a motivator, anger encourages you to pursue your goals. When things go wrong or don't flow as you expected, a feeling of anger runs out. It indicates that you've moved away from your desired objectives. Therefore, anger gives you the energy and strength to remove whatever prevents you from obtaining what you want.

It can also boost your optimism, helping you focus on what you hope to achieve rather than the pain, insult, or victimization. When you're angry, you can feel positive about your ability to change the situation, empowering you to take action and move from an undesirable position into a desirable one.

Reason #10: It Enhances Cooperation

If the anger you experience is justified, as is your response or behavior, the misunderstanding between both parties can be clarified, resulting in cooperation. The expression of anger communicates to others that you're unhappy with their behavior or perceive their actions to be unjust or unfair.

Anger shows others that it's important to listen to you and what makes you feel annoyed, and that it's wise to pay attention to your words. This is how anger makes you constructively challenge the other side.

When used correctly, constructive anger can make you feel powerful, and helps to propel you forward in getting what you want. It seems that even angry, destructive feelings can possess the life force of anger, which can propel you into action, help to enhance communication both in personal and professional relationships, and foster optimism, among other benefits.

Anger potentially provides the energy you might need to act toward certain goals or to correct challenging or unfair situations.

When anger arises, you feel a need to eliminate the threats to you or those you care for. In this context, the real purpose of anger management isn't to bottle up anger, but to understand the message behind the emotion and express it in a healthy way without losing control. By learning to display your anger in a healthy, constructive manner, you'll be willing to effectively communicate your desires and needs.

Over time, as you refine your skills for turning anger from a potentially destructive force into a constructive resource, you can expect to develop new insights into your feelings as well as those of others. The goal in learning how to handle anger is to minimize the negative consequences of this powerful emotion while maximizing the positive ones.

You can use anger to turn feelings of vulnerability and powerlessness into feelings of control and strength. Research has amply shown that feelings of anger enhance optimism, creativity, and effective work, and studies show that venting anger leads to better negotiations, whether in life or work. Lashing out when angry may cause feelings of guilt or lead to emotionally hurting others around you. If you let anger and other negative emotions overpower your positive feelings, you may find yourself consumed with bitterness or feelings of unfairness.

The phrase constructive anger might seem like an oxymoron, but actually, learning how to harness negative feelings in a positive manner can do much to aid in healing, forward motion, and recovery. The feedback that anger can provide is critical to social relationships, and actually may be the thing that makes them healthier, as long as anger isn't overly extreme.

Anger's Positive Effect on Mental Health

The way you process your angry expressions also impacts your overall mental well-being. Anger can serve as a powerful motivator, so certain anger expressions can also change the way those around you perceive you.[11] For example, during a business negotiation, those who seem angrier are usually in a better position to tilt the process in their favor. This type of anger can be an excellent negotiating tool used to persuade, close a deal, or enhance the negotiated position.

Anger gives you a sense of power and strong character, and can help you gain the respect of those involved and succeed in the process. When one party believes you're angry, they may be more willing to compromise.

The will to embrace uncomfortable emotions like anger instead of repressing them improves emotional intelligence. People who are emotionally intelligent use the wisdom that anger offers to make their lives better. Consequently, they have highly flexible emotional response systems, and are more resilient.

Anger can also lead to self-improvement, making you take action to change your shortcomings. When you know what triggers your anger, you can work on these factors to adjust your responses to them in a healthy way and, consequently, enhance the quality of your life and social interactions.

Many forces push anger to the surface; for example, defensiveness, or the fear of losing control, being alone, abandoned, or rejected. Anger then gives you access to a deeper self, the layers of which contain deeper issues that are mostly hidden. For this reason, it's important for you to trace the anger trail while addressing its origins. Only when you're capable of addressing the trigger of your anger can you remove any feeling of desolation and regret that comes with it.

However, many of these are short-term benefits, as many don't like to spend time with angry people due to its contagiousness.

THE BAD SIDE OF ANGER

Anger is metabolically demanding, being a draining and exhausting emotion. Sustaining angry feelings for long periods is complicated, because it's such a powerful emotion. After all, when you're angry, your brain experiences something closely related to stress, and stress is, of course, not good for you.

Furthermore, anger can be misused to assert control and bully others in a working environment or in personal relationships. On the other hand, others may deny having angry feelings because they're afraid or uncomfortable with feeling it.

Anger ranges in its level of intensity, from slight annoyance to rage, and can be excessive or irrational. Several studies on anger show how this emotion impacts us both physiologically and psychologically. Before anger affects any part of the body, it affects the brain. The brain processes all emotional stress.

When your brain senses a threat, millions of nerve fibers release chemicals to every organ. When a person experiences anger, the sympathetic nervous system in the brain invokes intense anger responses by overflowing the body with stress hormones, adrenaline, and noradrenaline, which help your body regulate the heart rate, blood pressure, and the pancreas that controls the sugar balance in your blood.[12]

Then the parasympathetic nervous system—the part of the body's nervous system whose function is to calm people—releases the hormone acetylcholine to stop the arousal of this emotion. Acetylcholine is in charge of neutralizing the stress hormones, and helps your body relax.

The constant flood of stress chemicals caused by unmanaged anger can eventually harm many different systems in your body. As the anger persists, it will also affect many of the body's systems, such as the cardiovascular, immune, digestive, and central nervous systems.[13]

Chronic long-term stress is associated with decreased immunity by increasing the risk of bronchial constriction, plaque buildup in the arteries, and too much acid in the stomach. Therefore, the manifestations of anger don't only express themselves in psychiatric symptoms, but may also result in chronic diseases related to the heart or digestive and immune systems; this is due to the arousal and hypervigilance associated with anger experiences, combined with the high cognitive and physiological resources needed to downregulate such chronic anger.[14]

These physiological reactions can lead to increases in cardiovascular responding, blood flow to active muscles, and strength. Overall, it will lead to increased risks of:

- severe headache
- reduced threshold for pain
- hypertension
- insomnia
- substance abuse
- chronic fatigue syndrome
- skin problems such as eczema and neurodermatitis (inflammations of the skin)
- digestion problems such as abdominal pain
- gastric ulcers
- bowel disease

- visceral and pain hypersensitivity
- type 2 diabetes
- strokes
- heart attack
- some types of cancer

Furthermore, chronic anger leads to psychological problems such as:

- depression
- anxiety
- epilepsy
- reduced self-confidence
- eating disorders
- alcoholism
- substance abuse
- self-injury
- aggressive behaviors toward others

Now we'll explore the main negative effects of anger outbursts.

Effect #1: Risk of Heart Disease

When you're angry, your breathing becomes more rapid because it's trying to get more oxygen to your brain. Anger can also affect circulation. If your body isn't getting enough oxygen, this can lead to chest pains, and can cause an artery to burst, resulting in a stroke. Scientists found that the connection between anger and hostility is significantly associated with heart disease.[15]

Repressed anger is linked to heart disease. People with anger proneness as a personality trait were at twice the risk for coronary disease than the general population.[16] In fact, two hours after an angry outburst, the chance of having a heart attack doubles.[17] This means that those with normal blood pressure but with high traits of anger, anger expression, chronic hostility, depression, or acute anger episodes can experience new and recurrent cardiovascular issues.[18]

Effect #2: Risk of Stroke

Anger increases your stroke risk. If you're prone to lashing out, beware. Research has found that there's a three times higher risk of having a stroke from a blood clot in the brain or bleeding within the brain during the two hours after an angry outburst; for example, for people with an aneurysm in one of the brain's arteries, there was a six times higher risk of rupturing this aneurysm following an angry outburst.[19]

Effect #3: Weak Immune System

Harvard University scientists found that when healthy people recall an angry experience from their past, it causes a six-hour dip in antibody immunoglobulin A, the cells' first line of defense against infection.[20]

Effect #4: Gastrointestinal Problems

Some emotions tend to be reflected in the stomach or digestive system. Anger control and suppression, based on cognitive and behavioral efforts to restrain angry feelings, are associated with prolonged gastric emptying and delayed gut transit.[21] Stress, as a reaction to anger, makes your stomach produce too much acid, which causes gastric ulcers and acid reflux; likewise, for those with irritated bowel syndrome, such kinds of emotions worsen the problem.[22]

Effect #5: Respiratory Problems

People with long, recurrent anger episodes have poor pulmonary functioning and experience higher decline rates as they age.

A group of scientists from Harvard University studied 670 men over eight years using a hostility scale scoring method to measure their anger levels and analyze any changes in their lung function. They concluded that the men with the highest hostility ratings had the worse lung capacity, which increased their risk of respiratory problems; the study shows that an uptick in stress hormones—associated with feelings of anger—creates inflammation in the airways.[23]

Effect #6: Anxiety

Difficulties dealing with anger can worsen your anxiety. As we discussed in Chapter 1, anxiety and anger can go hand-in-hand. It can also be damaging for those suffering from Generalized Anxiety Disorder (GAD), a condition characterized by excessive and uncontrollable worry. For the clinically anxious, anger can serve as a trigger that exacerbates symptoms.[24]

Effect #7: Depression

Several studies have linked depression with aggression and angry outbursts. Based on the equity theory, our perceptions of inequality in social roles foment feelings of anger and frustration. Feeling inferior and underestimated may yield some of the highest levels of anger, especially the type of anger that persists for a long time and contributes to episodic anger and angry moods, which lead to mental health outcomes like depression.[25]

Effect #8: Short Lifespan

Recurrent anger outbursts may shorten your lifespan. One of the studies conducted at the University of Michigan about anger found that couples who hold in their anger have a shorter life span than those who readily say when they're mad.[26]

Other Health Effects

Scientists have proven that chronic-angry people suffer frequent colds, infections, asthma, diabetes, skin disease flare-ups, and arthritis compared to non-chronic-angry people.[27]

Evidence also says that the daily experience of anger predicts elevated levels of chronic inflammation and associated illnesses. Anger can prolong stressful circumstances and facilitate a dysregulation of neuroendocrine processes in advanced old age, which could have significant implications for those who suffer from inflammatory processes and chronic illness, particularly in advanced old age.[28]

Anger doesn't cause you to have high cholesterol, but it aggravates the problem.[29] The chemical imbalance triggered by anger causes your metabolism to slow down, and feeling stressed and angry initiates excessive eating and weight gain.

Other consequences of uncontrolled anger include the risk of being a cigarette smoker and increased alcohol consumption. Evidence shows that this risk of smoking is 65% higher if you often experience intense anger. In contrast, the risk of suffering from alcoholism is 44%.[30] Also, anger is the second leading cause of relapse among ex-smokers, far less than stress or anxiety, but greater than depression.

HOW ANGER CAN DESTROY FAMILY RELATIONSHIPS

While anger is a common reaction to being treated badly or something in your life not going right, when you express it in ways that hurt you or others, it becomes an issue. Anger is a powerful emotion, and when not handled properly can lead to devastating outcomes for you and the people closest to you.

You may feel like the worst person when anger outbursts ruin the peace of the family or hurt loved ones. Every time I experienced anger episodes in my youth, my mom used to repeat to me that words, once said, cannot be taken back. She used the crumpled paper metaphor: "If you crumple a piece of paper and then smooth it out, you'll notice the creases remain, and that's what happens when you yell at us and release your frustration on your family. You leave small scars in our hearts."

The most intense emotional experiences occur in close, intimate bonds. People who are stressed and angry tend to alienate family and friends. Anger expressions in relationships can be detrimental. Lack of anger management leads not only to physical and mental issues, but also rifts in daily life, such as driving behavior, marriages, parent-child interactions, and the workplace.

Anger can hijack your ability to think clearly, leading to poor judgment and decision-making. Thus, anger is a common destroyer of relationships, but family members and couples usually underestimate or minimize its impact. For instance, average parents report high levels of anger towards their children, the need to engage in techniques to control their anger, and fear that they will lose control and harm their children.[31]

Anger within families then implies power struggles, which is the antithesis of support and cooperation. A house can become a battlefield, diminishing the trust family members have in each other. One of the worst experiences for a person to have is to shout at their parents during an angry outburst. When one exceeds such a limit and starts to destroy everything around them is when it's time to react and take action to solve the issue.

On the other hand, individuals who live together tend to share finite amounts of space and resources. To some degree, then, interpersonal conflict between members of the household is inevitable. Incompatibilities emerge in expectations and behaviors, from the trivial annoyances (such as who washes the dishes or cleans the room) to the more serious situations that incite anger (such as wrong behaviors, alcohol abuse, etc.).

Likewise, the parenthood role implies countless responsibilities that require energy and time, as well as increasing the affective exchange, stress, worries, frustration, and anger provocation. Although being a parent is an amazing experience, as it also provides opportunities to experience positive emotions, there are other elements that may cause sadness, annoyance, and anger.

Anger also underscores the importance of perceived threats to identity. One partner in an intimate relationship will seek to exert control over the other in order to restore identity verification. However, when the reassertion of control is unsuccessful, and deficits in identity verification remain, the risk increases for physical aggression "as a last resort" to reestablish control.[32]

Living with an angry person is very difficult, because this emotion is powerful enough to destroy any positive feelings that a couple has cultivated. Imagine for a few seconds having a marriage in which you often encounter conflicts; fights are a common issue, and your partner wastes their time and energy on negative behaviors. This situation is very frustrating.

Anger adversely affects how effectively you play your role as a spouse and parent. Studies show that the divorce rate for men and women who are ill-tempered is twice that of the average couple.[33] Anyone would refuse to suffer abusive anger from their mates.

Moreover, scientists found that hostile, irritable affective responses contributed to the link between economic hardship and negative outcomes in marital dyads, especially for men.[34] Criticism, anger, and threatening gestures in marital interactions ultimately influence perceptions about the quality of management and thoughts about marital dissolution, and potentially escalate into more serious forms of violence.

Raging anger often leads to violence, which makes people isolate themselves from family and friends. They experience low self-esteem, using their anger to manipulate their loved ones and feel powerful.

Anger also grows in relationships that are insecure and lack open communication. The emotion of love is buried under years and years of hostility and resentment. In these relationships, helplessness often exists in the present, and anxiety and fear are present in thoughts about the future.

The next chapter will present the most common types of anger expressions that show up in life, with methods on how to identify each one.

4

ANGER IN ALL ITS FORMS

When angry, count to ten before you speak. If very angry, count to one hundred.

— THOMAS JEFFERSON

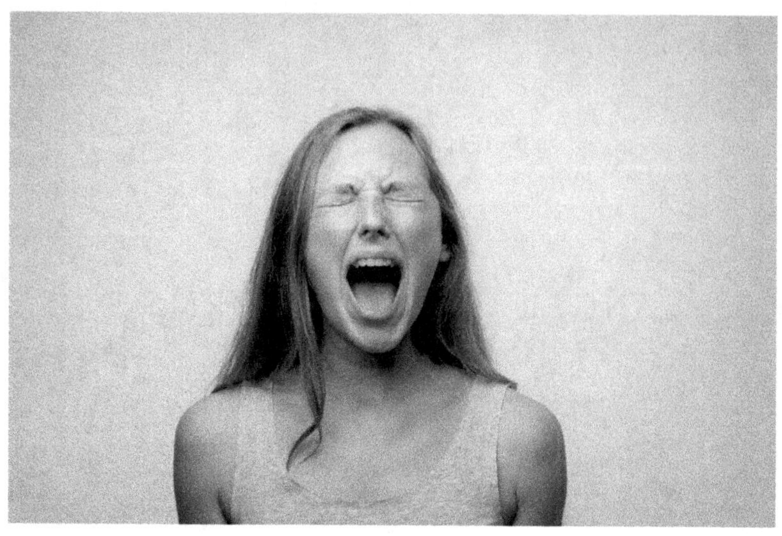

TYPES OF ANGER

There are plenty of other forms that anger can take, but these are the ones most people typically experience when they're feeling mad.

Assertive Anger

In this type of anger, frustration acts as a catalyst for positive change. Hence, it's a powerful motivator used to overcome fear, address injustice, and achieve more desired outcomes in life.

Anger is expressed in a constructive way instead of avoiding confrontation, internalizing the emotion, or using verbal insults and physical outbursts. You directly talk with the person or people you're angry with and handle the issue in a problem-solving manner.

Assertive anger may address your needs without transgressing others' rights and boundaries. This is a healthy option for expressing anger, as it involves handling anger in a non-threatening way by calmly explaining personal feelings and trying to diffuse the situation. Therefore, it isn't associated with a risk for heart disease.

The common triggers of this type of anger are emotional maturity, self-confidence, strong interpersonal skills, and highly valued relationships. Accordingly, implementing assertive anger techniques is only possible if the parties involved have enough emotional maturity, the nature of the situation is suitable, and the underlying relationship between the parties is strong or rooted in common values.

There are some signs that can indicate if your anger expressions fall under an assertive approach. These signs imply the understanding of emotions, challenges, and mature mechanisms to prevent anger from spiraling out of control. For instance:

- Communicating with confidence and respect when feeling angry.

- Respecting yourself and others, including their rights and opinions.
- Controlling your emotions while being empathetic to others' feelings.
- Understanding the impact of the other side's actions and concerns in the situation.
- Analyzing the cause of the problem to identify the trigger of the anger.
- Finding solutions to resolve the matter in a beneficial way for all parties involved.
- Willingness to forgive and ask for forgiveness.

When you assertively communicate your negative emotions and work towards a positive outcome, it helps you avoid the pitfalls of negative anger expressions. Likewise, you'll release unhealthy stress energy.

Behavioral Anger

Behavioral anger is a regular state of excessive anger, which has negative consequences for interpersonal relations. This is because this type of anger is triggered by unpredictable and impulsive behaviors that affect one's ability to build trusting and respectful relationships. Anger outbursts can also be associated with an exaggerated sense of frustration or injustice.

It implies behavioral aggression, which can lend itself to the most extreme end of the spectrum and turn violent. This includes breaking or throwing things in an angry outburst or physically intimidating or attacking someone. This type of anger expression is often explosive as it often spirals out of control, which can lead to words and actions you'll regret once you calm down.

This anger expression is common in both children and adults, and is usually accompanied by other psychological or behavioral issues, such as autism, depression, attention deficit disorder (ADD), anxiety disorder, post-traumatic stress disorder (PTSD), or bipolar disorder.

Studies found that intense and out-of-control anger outbursts may be of clinical concern in children. Moreover, anger outbursts from trivial provocations of daily life can persist during their development and manifest through some psychiatric disorders. Because of an apparent lack of control, these behaviors have been conceptualized as "rage attacks" in severe mood dysregulation and Tourette Syndrome (TS), as well as meltdowns in children on the autism spectrum.[1]

Several scientific studies have shown that irritability signs or symptoms during a person's childhood are linked to mood and anxiety disorders later in life, whereas defiance and vindictiveness predict later conduct problems.[2]

Among the signs of behavioral anger, one can observe:

- exaggerated responses to external stimuli
- being in a regular state of anger
- emotional or physical abuse
- using anger to obtain what one wants
- anger episodes that last for a long period and are out of proportion
- anger that affects outside situations
- alcohol or drug abuse
- increased blood pressure and heart rate when feeling mad

Chronic Anger

Chronic anger is often directed towards other people, situations, and even yourself, which not only affects your self-esteem, but also diminishes your capacity to get out of a difficult situation. It may feel like a permanent sense of frustration, alongside irritation, guilt, and resentment. This type of anger tends to increase with time.

This anger expression is triggered by different chronic stressors such as demands, conflicts, and threats under reward, complexity, and structural constraints. Scientists classify them as chronic, due to their correlation to enduring, persistent, and structured experiences in family, school, work, and neighborhood domains.[3]

Chronic anger can become an addiction that, without help, will cause severe damage to your physical and mental health, as well as destroy your relationships. It can lead to a negative mindset, causing frequent anger outbursts that increase over time.

Like behavioral anger, chronic anger can cause mental health issues such as personality disorder, bipolar disorder, and oppositional defiant disorder. However, this doesn't mean that all people who experience chronic anger have one of these mental health issues.

A variety of factors and circumstances can cause chronic anger, such as traumatic experiences, hereditary factors (Individuals who experience chronic anger may have children who also exhibit symptoms of it,) irregularities within the brain (Those who are afflicted with temporal lobe damage or temporal lobe epilepsy,) and environmental factors.

If a person displays more than one of the following symptoms, they could be experiencing chronic anger:

- increased anger throughout the day
- feeling anger that lasts for many months
- lack of respect for the law

- acts of physical violence or aggression
- lack of connection with others
- displays of road rage
- ongoing emotional detachment
- weak immune system

Destructive Anger

Destructive anger is a significantly unhealthy experience of anger that can have multiple adverse effects. It's linked to the extreme end of behavioral anger, including extreme irritability or even hatred of others.

Destructive anger implies verbal or physical actions that aim to hurt others. As its name indicates, this type of anger destroys many areas of your life, including the most critical social connections.

Unprocessed anger leads to conflict, social isolation, conflicts at work, substance abuse, depression, shame, and even incarceration. The signs are similar to those who experience chronic anger.

Judgmental Anger

This anger expression, also described as a "justified fury," often lowers your self-esteem. Those who display judgmental anger show negative emotions by humiliating or putting others down in public with the only purpose of making themselves look better or at an advantage. They always look for opportunities to criticize those around them by noticing their shortcomings. Although such anger makes the individual believe they're morally superior, it may create new nexus with similar people by invalidating their opinions and perspectives.

Overwhelmed Anger

Overwhelming anger alerts us to analyze what isn't going well and allows us to fix it. Being emotionally overwhelmed includes having mood swings, being upset or hurt, and being extremely stressed. It can also result in negative thoughts about certain people, events, or memories.

If we don't control it, this anger causes us trouble at work or school, difficulties managing stress, conflicts in friendships and relationships, difficulty relating to others, substance abuse, physical or emotional outbursts, muscle pain, insomnia, anxiety, and depression.

Passive-Aggressive Anger

Passive anger is the opposite of aggressive anger, because the behaviors it embraces lead to acting indirectly aggressive rather than directly aggressive. When an individual represses their anger because they don't want to cope with it, eventually their anger finds an unhealthy and undermining way to burst out. In this situation, you try to evade all forms of confrontation and may deny or repress any feelings of fury or rage you're experiencing.

Passive-aggressive behavior may be expressed verbally as sarcastic comments, backhanded compliments, pointed silence, mockery, or acts of unconscious aggression against the person you're mad at. It can be expressed physically through behaviors such as chronic procrastination at work or in studies.

This type of anger can also be directed internally, so if you've repressed your anger so much, you may not notice you're angry. The main signs of this anger expression include repeatedly making excuses to avoid certain people—aiming at expressing dislike towards those individuals, rejecting the demands of their family or others by procrastinating (a sense of carelessness), acting stubborn, and refusing to admit to being angry or sharing your feelings.

Retaliatory Anger

Retaliatory anger is an instinctual reaction to being attacked by an external situation or person. As a consequence, it's considered one of the most common types of anger. Retaliatory anger is fueled by a negative reaction to others and revenge for a perceived wrong. It often occurs in a family context and can be one of the most destructive and dangerous anger disorders.

Such vengeful rage is also deliberate, and often aims to intimidate others by asserting control over a situation or outcome, although it only exacerbates tensions. Retaliation is a choice, not an impulse, so it disappears once you decide it's enough.

The most common causes of retaliatory anger are:

- long periods of stress and worry
- difficulties dealing with family, friends, or co-workers regularly
- poor impulse control
- alcohol and drug abuse
- exhaustion
- underlying psychological and mental health issues such as depression, obsessive-compulsive personality disorder, or narcissistic personality disorder
- intermittent explosive disorder

The signs and outcomes associated with retaliatory anger are:

- turning a minor problem into a major issue
- avoiding stepping back from reacting with anger
- a pattern of anger control issues
- emotions, thoughts, or out-of-control actions

Self-Abusive Anger

Self-abusive anger is rooted in feelings of self-shame and lack of self-esteem. When feeling hopeless, unworthy, humiliated, or ashamed, you might internalize these feelings and express your rage via negative self-talk, self-blaming, self-harm, substance abuse, or disordered eating. Likewise, you might lash out at those around you to mask feelings of low self-worth, ultimately increasing your sense of alienation.

It consists of abusive relationships with ourselves and ways in which we can actively undermine our self-esteem and success. If we can't recognize the emotional violence, it can perpetuate a self-destructive dynamic.

Silent Anger

Also known as "repressed anger," it refers to anger that is unconsciously ignored, denied, or pushed down to avoid uncomfortable feelings related to stress, conflict, and tension. Those who experience it remain quiet. Most of the time, silent anger foments the symptoms of mental health issues linked to anxiety and depression. When not properly treated, it may cause low self-esteem, a self-sabotaging tendency, physical pain, and relationship conflicts.

It can occur due to traumatic experiences in childhood, experiencing trauma, limited emotional intelligence, medical conditions, high levels of shame, wanting to please others, and even cultural norms. In some cases, the person doesn't want to feel or talk about their anger. Likewise, many genetic and environmental factors can also trigger it.

The signs of silent anger include:

- being often sad or depressed, without showing anger
- avoidance of facing difficult emotions
- being sarcastic or overusing cynicism
- being uncomfortable with any kind of conflict or confrontation
- being defensive when someone accuses them of being angry
- feeling the need to control everything

- experiencing chronic muscle tension or headaches
- feeling uncomfortable when listening to the intimate emotions of others
- being passive-aggressive when interacting with others
- having difficulty setting boundaries, standing up for oneself, or saying no
- avoiding people or isolating when upset
- complaining when things don't go their way
- high levels of chronic stress and anxiety
- frequent self-critical thoughts and comments
- feeling envious and resentful of others
- ignoring anger triggers rather than addressing them
- ruminating on bad experiences
- feeling guilty or ashamed when angry

Such anger expression may lead to many negative outcomes for physical and mental health, damaging your quality of life. These can include chronic stress, heart problems, insomnia, lowered self-esteem, apathy, anxiety, depression, higher risk of addiction, impulsivity and self-destructive behaviors, lack of concentration, less open and honest communication, poor relationships, and impaired work performance.

By learning to assimilate and vent feelings of anger in a healthy way, you can find the tools to positively impact your life in many ways.

Volatile Anger

Volatile or irrational anger embraces an episode of extreme anger that appears suddenly without warning. It puts individuals at risk of self-harm, property damage, violence toward others, and interpersonal problems. The long-term nature of volatile anger has a profoundly negative impact on one's health and well-being, causing chronic sleep disorders, stroke, and memory loss.

Emotional symptoms are not limited to anger; they may also include anxiety, irritability, and rage. Those who experience this anger have muscle pain and tension, dizziness, poor memory and concentration, nausea, headaches, and rapid breathing. Mental health experts affirm this form of anger should never be acceptable.

Clarifying what you believe about emotions, identifying your anger patterns and their different types of expressions, and learning strategies to manage your anger problems are the keys to opening the door to healthy expression of emotions that will help you get your needs met without upsetting others.

With practice, you can curb any tendencies toward verbal aggression and replace them with assertive anger expressions. Rather than avoiding confrontation, repressing your anger, or using verbal insults and physical lash-outs, anger is displayed in ways that bring about constructive change that get you closer to having your needs met without creating hurt or disruption.

As long as it's expressed in an appropriate manner, a kind of healthy anger is empathy anger, or justifiable indignation. Another type of healthy anger is incidental anger, or anger at a particular event or situation that's addressed directly and rapidly.

The next chapter will give readers the details of bottling up and erupting emotions.

5

BOTTLING UP AND ERUPTIONS

Anger is a tool for change when it challenges us to become more of an expert on the self and less of an expert on others.

— HARRIET LERNER

BOTTLING UP YOUR ANGER

Bottling up emotions consists of keeping what we feel inside us, an approach that prevents us from discussing our needs and connecting with others. It can carry on unexpected consequences for mental and physical health in the long-term.

You may tend to suppress your emotions under certain circumstances; when you're overwhelmed by daily worries and don't want to give importance to the emotion; when you prefer to hide your feelings to avoid more problems in your relationship; or just don't have the time to deal with it, and it seems easier and safer not to do so.

There's a misconception that sharing your emotions makes you vulnerable. According to some psychologists, people bottle up their emotions due to a fear of vulnerability, which provides a false sense of emotional safety. Out of this fear, they react through self-protective emotional measures.[1]

Among the causes of bottled-up anger are irritability, internal restlessness, sadness, and frustration. Even so, triggers for each person vary. Factors such as feeling unheard or unappreciated, lack of acceptance of a situation, and unmet needs are included among these triggers.[2]

Most of us don't realize that we're bottling up our deepest emotions. Therefore, pay attention to whether you experience any of these symptoms:

- growing irritability and frustration towards everything and everyone
- poor sleep or insomnia
- digestive problems, headaches, racing heartbeats, and muscle tension
- increased feelings of resentment
- feeling on edge
- criticizing or hurting others

CONSEQUENCES OF BOTTLING UP YOUR ANGER

First, chronic dismissal of your emotions ultimately impacts self-confidence. You may eventually complain that nobody cares about your needs or desires. In some cases, you may even feel deeply enraged and develop feelings of resentment toward others. Likewise, depression and anxiety are examples of unexpressed anger, because anger turned inward often results in self-hatred.[3]

Second, it compromises your physical health because it can lead to physical stress on the body. The stress caused to your body can increase the risk of diabetes and heart disease.[4] Authors such as Giora Keinan found that, in terms of health, the best thing to do is to get very angry, marking your position "clearly and firmly," but not too often. He suggests that those who do this tend to be the same people who are good at finding other ways of dealing with problems, which reduces the amount of stress they experience and improves immune function, leading to better overall health.[5]

Third, bottling up anger affects your social relationships. If you don't adequately express yourself, your relationships can't grow in meaningful ways, as people expect honesty from you.

Nevertheless, a study from the University of North Carolina in 2000 concluded that those who frequently lose their temper are three times more likely to have had heart attacks than people who don't. Similarly, Professor Mark McDermott from the University of East London found that people who express their anger suffer more from heart disease than those who hold it in.[6]

Based on these studies, expressing anger may be problematic, because when you get angry your body gets ready for the fight-or-flight response and may take fat from smooth muscle if you need extra energy. If these acids aren't used, the body sends them somewhere else; they often go to the artery walls directly, forming deposits that can cause heart disease. Likewise, your blood pressure increases when you lose your temper, and can leave tiny injuries inflicted on the coronary artery walls. If these issues occur often, the consequences can worsen in the future.

These statements try to explain that expressing anger in an unhealthy way can bring negative consequences, not that bottling up anger is the best option to handle it. Therefore, it all depends on how you express your anger. If you express your anger constructively, for a justified purpose, you're less likely to suffer cardiovascular disease. But, if you express it to blame others and justify your actions, the risk of heart disease increases. In conclusion, occasional outbursts are sometimes necessary for feeling release. Although, on top of that, what really matters is how you get angry, and how often.

PREVENT BOTTLED-UP ANGER

Let's discuss some helpful tips that will guide you to prevent bottled-up anger:

- *Assess your environment.* Understanding the source of anger helps you cope with the situation or the persons involved. A way to achieve this is by analyzing your environment and making changes if necessary.
- *Add exercise to your routine.* Working with your body is very useful in dealing with anger since it's a way to match its intensity and safely ride its wave. Physical activity is an excellent strategy for not only keeping your body healthy, but also your mind. Exercise has countless benefits; among them are helping you deal with anger, decompress, reduce stress, and burn off any extra tension in your life. It isn't necessary to be a slave to the gym—30 minutes

of biking, walking, or running four times a week is an excellent start.

- ***Improve your mindset.*** Psychologists recommend applying cognitive restructuring to replace negative thoughts with positive or more reasonable ones. This doesn't mean you should force yourself to think differently or challenge yourself to decide whether you're acting rationally or irrationally. The main purpose is to gradually change your attitude towards your feelings and thoughts. This mental shift helps you slow down what you think, put everything in perspective, and change your problems into solutions.

- ***Practice self-talk.*** The words you say to yourself are very powerful and influence how you feel and behave. You should have an inner dialogue that can put you in a calmer frame of mind. I always repeat to myself as soon as I wake up: "It's a new day, a new opportunity to learn and enjoy life!" Likewise, I replace phrases like "I can't change how I feel" and "They make me angry" with "I can control my emotions" and "When they do [something I don't like], I choose to think [something more optimistic]," respectively.

- ***Practice relaxation techniques.*** Exercises such as deep breathing and guided meditation play a key role in controlling anger. Both help you to release your body and mind when experiencing anger (we'll explore these techniques in the following chapters.)
- ***Keep a healthy diet.*** It's been proven that food has a considerable impact on our mood. Therefore, you should reduce your consumption of high amounts of sugar, processed foods, and refined carbohydrates. It's also necessary to avoid alcohol and drugs. These substances can increase the risk of violent behaviors.
- ***Get good sleep.*** Lack of good sleep has a huge impact on how you feel and how well you cope with things that happen to you daily.
- ***Build emotional resilience.*** It helps you handle difficult emotions and prevent anger outbursts when they're about to happen.
- ***Find some hobbies.*** The modern lifestyle can keep us busy, but there's always time to do what we enjoy. Listening to music, reading, practicing sports, dancing, and writing are excellent tools to express those intense and challenging emotions.

ANGER ERUPTIONS

Explosive Anger

Different types of anger disorders can cause angry behavior; among them is intermittent explosive disorder (IED).

Intermittent explosive disorder is a mental health condition that can start during childhood and continue on into adulthood. People with this disorder have a low tolerance for frustration and adversity, although they behave normally outside of hostile outbursts. In this case, aggressive episodes include increased energy, palpitations, rage, irritability, racing thoughts, tremors, tingling, and chest tightness.[7]

Aggressive outbursts are impulsive and happen rapidly after being provoked. They often don't last more than 20-30 minutes. In this case, anger manifests through temper tantrums, verbal arguments (shouting, heated arguments, and threatening others), physically assaulting people or animals (shoving, slapping, punching, or using a weapon to cause harm), property or object damage (kicking or breaking objects and slamming doors), domestic violence, and road rage.[8]

These episodes can occur very often or every few weeks to months, causing significant distress and conflicts at school, work, or home. In addition, the disorder commonly affects children around six years old and adults (mostly male) younger than 40 years old. Scientists estimate that between 1.4% and 7% of people have intermittent explosive disorder. Studies have also found that about 80% of people with IED have other mental health conditions involving anxiety disorders, bipolar disorder, externalizing disorder, intellectual disabilities, and autism.[9]

Researchers consider that genetic, biological, and environmental factors contribute to the development of IED.[10] First, this disorder more commonly runs in biological families. Studies suggest that 44% to 72% of the likelihood of developing impulsive aggressive behavior is genetic.[11]

Second, intermittent explosive disorder alters the brain's structure and function. For instance, brain magnetic resonance imaging (MRI) studies indicate that it affects the amygdala. Studies also show that serotonin is lower in people with IED.[12] Likewise, those who have an antisocial personality disorder, borderline personality disorder, or any other mental issue that includes disruptive behaviors such as attention-deficit/hyperactivity disorder (ADHD) have a higher risk of having intermittent explosive disorder.[13]

Third, experiencing or witnessing verbal and physical abuse or traumatic events during childhood can play a crucial role in developing IEDs. Being exposed to this environment at an early age, individuals become more likely to exhibit similar behaviors and treat others aggressively as they mature.

The Signs of Explosive Anger

In order to treat explosive anger on time, it's necessary to recognize the signs of the intermittent explosive disorder, either in yourself or in others, to address the issue properly:

- **High irritability.** This means having difficulty overcoming stressful and frustrating situations and thoughts. When this happens very often, the person feels as though their needs haven't been met, and therefore needs to release their frustration through bursts of anger.

- ***Intense anger.*** This type of anger is one of the earlier symptoms of IED. We already discussed in previous chapters that everyone experiences anger at different levels and degrees, but when it gets dangerous and recurrent is when anger rises to an extreme, especially when trivial and minor issues trigger the reaction. In children, for example, the signs include having temper tantrums or hitting objects, peers, or parents. Adults with anger problems also hit objects and people, or damage properties. In the case of children and young adults, anger is a problem when they can't control their anger, their thoughts are constantly negative, they threaten violence to themselves or others, or feel compelled to do dangerous, harmful things to release their anger.

- ***Mood changes before an outburst.*** People who experience mood swings, especially those with anxiety or anger disorders, tend to be diagnosed with IED. Feeling overwhelmed with emotions like disappointment, stress, or frustration may lead you into an explosive episode.

- ***Uncontrollable rage.*** This is one of the most severe symptoms of intermittent explosive disorder. This causes people to do extreme, regrettable things such as hurting others or themself or destroying property to release their anger. A person with IED may recognize feeling entirely out of control of their situation and emotions before erupting into physical and verbal violence.

- ***Guilt.*** After an intensive anger episode, a person with an IED may feel guilty and embarrassed, regardless of how significant the situation was. Although individuals with IED are aware that their behaviors are inappropriate, they feel like they can't control their actions during anger episodes. It proves that people with such disorders aren't bad or evil; they do bad things because they can't control themselves or don't know how to cope with it.

In general, people with intermittent explosive disorder have poor life satisfaction and a lower quality of life, as it impacts not only overall health but also personal and professional relationships. People with intermittent explosive disorder develop some of the following conditions: physical health problems, anxiety disorders, depression, alcohol or substance use disorder, and an increased risk for self-injury or even suicide.[14]

Regarding physical health problems, those who experience explosive anger have certain medical conditions, such as high blood pressure, heart disease, stroke, diabetes, ulcers, and chronic pain. Furthermore, depression is marked by persistent sadness and a lack of interest in everyday life and people. Those who feel depressed after an episode say they have difficulty completing regular tasks at home, school, or the office; they don't have any interest in things they often enjoy, and may feel fatigued or suffer insomnia.

The symptoms of such mental health conditions may decrease over time and with age, but the only way to be adequately treated is with medication and psychotherapy. Consequently, if you suspect you or any member of your family have any of these symptoms, you must talk to your healthcare provider or directly to a licensed mental health professional.

Managing Explosive Anger

The American Psychological Association (APA) recommends a series of strategies to manage explosive anger[15]:

Tip #1: Check Yourself

You must assess your emotions and behaviors and recognize the warning signs that you're getting angry or annoyed by someone or something. It'll help you take action when detecting them and step away from the situation, preventing your anger from escalating. I know it's hard to think clearly under such strong emotions, but try to first talk yourself down and then use some relaxation techniques.

Tip #2: Cognitive Restructuring

We mentioned this technique in the previous section. It refers to learning how to analyze aversive situations appropriately. It'll help if you work on those negative thoughts linked to frustrating events. An excellent way to do it is by developing rational thoughts and expectations, so your logic and critical thinking will improve the way you see and react to similar events in the future.

For instance, every day try to tell yourself positive words or statements such as "this is disappointing, but I can handle it." Avoid words like 'never,' 'always,' or 'everyone,' as they distort the way you interpret the situation and make you feel powerless.

Tip #3: Don't Dwell on the Anger

Some of us tend to keep rehashing the incident that made us angry, but this isn't the proper manner to handle it in, especially if you've already resolved the issue. You must avoid this vicious circle. Instead, forget the incident and focus on the lesson you obtained from the experience that made you angry.

Tip #4: Use Problem Solving

Another strategy is to design a plan to solve the frustrating problem. Even if you can't fix it right away, having a plan can refocus your energy.

Tip #5: Learn to Relax

There are countless experiences to help you stay relaxed. In Chapter 6 we'll discuss some of them, but here are the most common ones: Practicing exercises such as deep breathing or even yoga regularly may help you stay calm. For example, focused breathing and the visualization of a relaxing experience from your memory or imagination help you slow your breathing and relax your mind. Another helpful technique is progressive muscle relaxation, where you gradually tense and relax each muscle one at a time.

Tip #6: Improve Your Communication skills

This strategy is crucial when your anger is directed towards others, because you can share your feelings without hurting anyone. In a frustrating circumstance, you should try to listen to the message others are sharing with you before reacting; then, think about the best response rather than saying the first idea that comes to your mind. Take the time you need to analyze the situation with a clear and fresh mind, and avoid negative communication.

This is the reason why we have two ears and just one mouth. Think twice before speaking. Finally, effectively communicate your message with a soft voice and positive body language.

Tip #7: Stay Active

One of the best ways to improve your mental health is through regular physical activity. It helps release extra tension in your body and reduce the stress that feeds angry outbursts.

Tip #8: Follow Medical Treatment

In case you're under psychological treatment, it's important to be disciplined with therapy sessions. Regularly practice your coping skills, and if your doctor prescribes medication to avoid recurrent anger episodes, remember to take it.

The following few chapters will begin delving into physical and mental exercises for anger management.

6

ANGER EXERCISES – RELAXATION

If you are patient in one moment of anger, you will escape a hundred days of sorrow.

— CHINESE PROVERB

RELAXATION TECHNIQUES

Anger frequently manifests in muscle tension, and this tension can mainly accumulate in your face, neck, chest, and shoulders, and remain long after the anger has gone. Therefore, in anger management, relaxation is the key to controlling yourself before negative emotions run out.

Relaxation exercises regulate your fight-or-flight response and heal your body, making it come back into balance. These practices also give you the time you need to assess the situation that upset you, which will help you generate realistic and proper solutions to the problem. See the following relaxation techniques that can help you to stay calm and stop focusing on being angry.

One more important thing: If you have a respiratory disease or condition, you must talk to a doctor or respiratory therapist before practicing these exercises.

Breathing Exercises

Breathing is an unconscious action, but we can bring it under conscious control to make a positive impact on your body. Breathing exercises are designed to bring your body into deep relaxation. They have specific patterns that involve holding the breath for a few seconds to allow your body to refill its oxygen.

We already discussed that both breathing and heart rate increase when your emotions become out of control. It's possible to reverse these increases by consciously slowing your breathing and relaxing your muscles. As every part of our bodies are connected, we can make our heart rate slow down and reduce the tension in our muscles as we control our breath.

Finally, as you're practicing for relaxation, avoid doing it before an activity that requires your maximum attention and energy, like driving, cooking, working, or studying.

Exercise #1: 4-7-8 Breathing

The 4-7-8 breathing technique is a strategy based on an ancient yogic pattern called *pranayama* ("control of energy" in Sanskrit), which helps you control your breathing and calms your nervous system. The 4-7-8 technique makes your mind and body only focus on regulating your breath rather than your worries.

From the lungs outward, such a technique can give your organs and tissues a much-needed oxygen boost. Another of its benefits is that, when practiced regularly, it can help you fall asleep faster.

Now, here are the steps. Keep in mind that all of these steps should be carried out in the cycle of one breath:

1. Find a peaceful spot to sit or lie down comfortably in your bed. Maintain a good posture during the exercise (If you do it before going to bed, lie down in a comfortable position.)
2. Place the tip of the tongue against the roof of the mouth, behind the top front teeth. Try to keep the tongue in that position during the exercise; it can be challenging initially, but with practice, you can master it.
3. Let your lips part and exhale through your mouth.

4. Then, close your lips, inhaling silently through your nose as you count to four mentally. The air should go to your belly first and then to your chest. You can feel your ribs expand as your lungs do.

5. Hold your breath for seven seconds.

6. Exhale from your mouth for eight seconds while concentrating on where the air in your lungs is moving to. Also, notice how your ribs return to their original location as you exhale completely.

7. When inhaling again, you'll initiate a new breath cycle.

Furthermore, as a pro-tip, you should try to coordinate your head movements with your breathing. For example, slowly roll your head to one side as you exhale, back to the center as you inhale, and to the other side as you exhale again.

Practice this pattern for at least four breathing cycles twice a day to obtain better results. Over time, you'll be able to do up to eight cycles each time. You can also combine this technique with some elements such as earplugs, relaxing music, and diffusing essential oils like lavender, among others.

Exercise #2: Alternate-Nostril Breathing

Alternate-nostril breathing is another type of yoga breathing practice—also known as *Nadi shodhana*—whose function is to relax your mind and body while reducing stress. This technique focuses on breathing through alternate nostrils, one side at a time. Researchers have found that practicing this exercise for 10 minutes brings more benefits, including regulating the nervous system, lowering anxiety, healing your body after a stress response, lowering blood pressure, and improving your sleep.[1]

Moreover, studies show that after one month, this technique may improve your breathing. You'll have better oxygen flow, and those who can exhale high amounts have healthy lungs; thus, alternate-nostril breathing can make the lung muscles stronger. Such breathing can also help to clear secretions in your lungs like mucus, making room for more oxygen and lowering your blood lactate levels, a chemical linked to panic attacks.[2]

The steps for this practice are:

1. Find a comfortable and quiet place, without any distractions.
2. Sit on a comfortable chair that supports your arms and legs.

3. Place your right hand on your nose, with your thumb on the right nostril, while moving your forefinger and middle finger out of the way.
4. Next, close your eyes and slowly exhale through your left nostril.
5. Once you have fully exhaled, release your right nostril and place your ring finger on the left nostril.
6. Slowly breathe in from the right side and make sure your breath is smooth and continuous.
7. Once you've fully inhaled, exhale through the right nostril.
8. Now move your ring finger out of the way and close the right nostril with your thumb again. Inhale and exhale through the left nostril.
9. Repeat the previous steps three times or more.
10. Soft music can help you with this exercise (I have specific songs to get my anger and frustration out.)

Exercise #3: Coherent Breathing

Coherent breathing consists of adjusting the length of time you spend on each phase of breathing: inhaling and exhaling. It's an easy way to reduce stress and calm down when feeling anxious.

Coherent breathing consists of taking long, deep breaths, five per minute. The objective is to extend the length of the inhale and exhale to about six seconds (or longer if your torso is longer). Such a type of deep breathing helps calm your body due to its positive effects on the autonomic nervous system.

Coherent breathing can also be helpful in boosting your energy and improving your sleep, immune system response, alertness, concentration, depressive symptoms, and managing stress and post-traumatic stress disorder. Indeed, according to some studies, the levels of gamma-aminobutyric acid (GABA)—an acid with anti-anxiety effects—can increase when practicing this type of breathing. Similarly, another study found that cytokines—small proteins associated with inflammation and stress—can decrease after coherent breathing.[3]

How to practice it?

1. Focus on your normal breaths and calculate how much time you take to inhale and exhale to get a baseline.
2. Find a comfortable position. Then, put one hand on your stomach.
3. Breathe in for about four seconds and then exhale for four seconds, but don't force the breath, do it naturally. Do this for one minute.

4. Repeat, but now extend your inhales and exhales to five seconds.

5. Do the same as before but extend further to six seconds.

6. Once you can do this for five minutes, gradually work up to 20 minutes.

You can practice this technique anytime, anywhere. During this exercise, be sure you're breathing from the diaphragm, and concentrate on mentally counting the length of your breaths. You can also extend the time of your breathing phases up to 10 if you feel in good condition to do it.

Visualization Exercises

When you continue to rethink, reconsider, and relive an incident that provoked your anger, you're ruminating. Rumination doesn't have any benefit, and only intensifies your irritation because the more you think and talk about it, the angrier you become. Now we'll explore some exercises to help you let go of your anger.

Exercise #1: Imagery

Imagery is about visualization. You just need a few minutes of positive imagery to release anger in that short interval. In the process, you're keeping away the events or circumstances that trigger your anger. Here's how to do it:

1. Find a private, quiet spot.
2. Rate your level of anger on a scale from 1 (mildly irritated) to 10 (extreme rage).
3. Close your eyes to stop visualizing what's in front of you in your external environment.
4. Let your hold on reality go and enter into the world of visualization. You have to grant yourself permission to let go of the things that provoked your anger, and the emotion itself.

5. Imagine something happy and cheerful. Feel free to imagine whatever you want, except the situations or people that make you angry.
6. Be specific during the process. Imagine who, what, and where; picture every aspect of the situation you chose, colors, shapes, etc. The more specific you are, the more engaged you are.
7. Hold that image for at least five minutes.
8. Re-evaluate your anger level. If it hasn't lowered, you may need a few more minutes of positive imagery, but don't give up.
9. Enjoy the sensation in your mind and body before coming back to reality.
10. Open your eyes and continue with your daily activities.

Exercise #2: The Balloon Visualization

The balloon visualization is an exercise where you pretend to hold a colored balloon. During the process, you must focus on the tensions in your fist, arms, and shoulders. These balloons represent the challenges, stresses, and tough aspects of your life that you want to let go of. What you need to do is:

1. Find a quiet space and sit comfortably.
2. Take a few minutes to clear your mind.
3. Close your eyes and imagine a picture of you with a balloon. Choose the color you consider most appropriate for your emotions.
4. Slowly inhale through your nose.
5. Next, slowly exhale through your mouth, blowing up the balloon with thoughts of stress,

negativity, anxiety, and tension until it's huge and full.

6. Then, release the balloon into the sky.
7. Repeat this process for several minutes until you feel calm, centered, and more optimistic. The key is to continue looking up at the skyline until you can no longer see the balloon.

The purpose of this exercise is to connect yourself to where you have stored the negativity, and breathe into it so that it can change. The ultimate goal of visualization is to allow the safe shift of anger from your body, as anger can become toxic very quickly.

Muscle Relaxation Exercises

The excess muscle tension caused by anger episodes is a waste of energy, contributes to fatigue, and can result in chronic pain. It's been scientifically proven that physical relaxation enhances mental relaxation; therefore, I'll explain some exercises that will benefit both your body and your mind.

Exercise #1: General Muscle Relaxation

Muscle relaxation is a simple exercise for calming the body in response to stress and worry. When you learn to systematically relax your muscles, you gain an important tool to deal with daily challenges. The following steps will make it easier for you to learn to properly release tension from your muscles:

1. Take a deep breath, make a tight fist with your right hand and hold it for three seconds. Then open your hand, releasing all the tension in it.

2. Do the same with the muscles in your face, tensing and relaxing them one by one. Add tension on the inhale, then exhale and let the muscle ease:

> *a. Forehead.* First, frown as if you're angry or puzzled, then exhale and smooth it out.
> *b. Eyes.* Screw up your eyes and exhale to release the tension.
> *c. Jaw and cheeks.* Clench your teeth and jaw, then exhale and relax.

3. Now, work on the muscles in your torso:

> *a. Shoulders.* Bunch up your shoulders while inhaling and let them slacken while you exhale.
> *b. Chest.* Take a deep, long inhale, tightening the chest muscles. Then let the tension go on the exhale.
> *c. Abdomen.* Tighten your belly as if someone's about to punch you, then relax. You'll feel a spread of warmth throughout your torso.

4. It's time now to relax your arms. Make a fist with both hands, tightening the biceps, triceps, and forearms, and let the tension drain out of them.

5. Finally, tense and relax your legs. Curl your toes up while tightening your thighs and calves before releasing the tension. At this point, you can feel what remains of the tension in your body dissipate.

Practice these exercises twice a day, and once finished, sit quietly for about 10 minutes. Don't practice in bed.

Exercise #2: Progressive Muscle Relaxation (PMR)

This exercise, also known as Jacobson's relaxation technique, is a kind of therapy that consists of tightening and relaxing your muscles in a specific pattern, one at a time. The main objective is to help you release the tension in your body and be aware of what that tension feels like.

Adopting PMR as a regular practice can help you handle the physical outcomes of stress. Scientific studies have proven that PMR has therapeutic benefits for those who suffer migraines, high blood pressure, and insomnia. It also reduces the symptoms of temporomandibular joint (a condition that leads to stiffness and locking of the jaw), depression, anxiety, and stress. It reduces neck and lower back pain while improving overall well-being and quality of life.[4]

In order to succeed in this practice, all you need is willingness, concentration, and a quiet environment where you won't be distracted. Let's explore the following steps:

1. Start by lying or sitting down. Do this in a quiet, comfortable area. Also turn off your phone to avoid distractions.
2. Then relax your entire body and take five deep breaths.
3. Lift your toes upward, hold, and then let go. Curl your toes downward, hold, and slacken.
4. Tense your calf muscles, then relax them.
5. Move your knees toward each other, hold, and slacken.
6. Squeeze the thigh muscles, hold, and slacken.
7. Clench your hands, hold, and slacken.
8. Tense your arms, hold, and then ease.
9. Contract your abdominal muscles, hold, and slacken.
10. Inhale and tighten your chest, pause for a few seconds, exhale, and slacken.
11. Bunch your shoulders up to your ears, pause, and slacken.
12. Open your mouth wide, hold, and then close it.
13. Close your eyes tightly, hold, and then open them.

The key to this exercise is to tense each muscle group and pause or hold for about five seconds. After that, exhale to let your muscles fully slacken for about 15 seconds before you move on to the next muscle group. Avoid holding your breath, which can cause more tension. Finally, deeply inhale while tensing your muscles; then fully exhale to relax.

As a beginner, it's better to practice PMR even when you're calm, since this will make it easier for you to learn the method. Try to use your imagination and let it take you to a happier moment in your life or a more peaceful setting.

The next chapter will continue exploring excellent physical exercises for anger management that will help the body relax and build awareness.

7

ANGER EXERCISES – THE BODY

Speak when you are angry, and you'll make the best speech you'll ever regret.

— AMBROSE BRIERCE

WORKOUT EXERCISES

Exercise, especially aerobics, helps you reduce anxiety and hostility while preventing an irritable mood. However, some people may have difficulty giving their time and energy to any physical activity when anger runs out. There are different ways to approach a workout in case of having a bad mood.

Before exploring some body exercises, keep in mind that such activities don't remove your anger, but are means for healthy anger expression and management.

Exercise #1: Boxing

Boxing is an exercise of focus, self-control, and self-discipline. Doing high-intensity boxing workouts like hitting a punching bag helps you channel uncontrolled anger and avoid negative feelings. When you practice boxing, your concentration improves, as you must focus on specific punch and jab combinations, avoiding unnecessary distractions.

Furthermore, this exercise makes you feel relaxed and in high spirits, as your brain increases endorphin production, one of the happiness hormones. Eventually, following a workout routine will enhance your self-esteem and overall mental strength to face real-life challenges.

Basic Boxing Workouts

- *Punching a boxing bag.* This is wonderfully liberating because you release loads of tension and energy through it. Start punching a bag at least three times a week, or whenever you feel overwhelmed, for ten minutes or more, and then combine it with some meditation or relaxation techniques. If you're a beginner, only focus on straight punching, alternating your hands left-right.
- *Sumo squat.* In this exercise, stand with your feet far apart and toes pointing out. Keep your back straight. Push your body up and down with the help of the heels while grasping your

hands together at chest level. When going down, crouch until your thighs are parallel to the floor. Do 15 repetitions three times a week.

- **Arm circles.** Stand in an upright position and open your arms out wide, forming a 'T'. Next, make circles with your arms, and move forwards and backwards. You can do this before the punching workout, as it warms up your back and shoulders.
- **Knee hugs.** Lying on your back with your knees bent, put your hands around one knee and draw it towards your chest, holding it for around 20 seconds before releasing it. Next, do the same with the other knee. Finally, repeat the exercise, drawing both knees in at the same time. You can also practice this exercise by standing in an upright position.
- **Quad stretch.** While standing, bend the right knee and hold your foot from the backside with your right hand. After that, slightly press your right hip forward. Repeat it with the left knee.

Exercise #2: Jump Rope

Jumping rope is a simple but entertaining exercise that requires foot coordination and has a huge impact on your emotional and physical well-being. A jump rope workout also helps you develop a meditative mindset to concentrate on which feelings are disturbing you and how to address them. Therefore, this exercise will help you overcome stress, anger, and anxiety.

Here are some tips when practicing jumping rope:

1. Start by finding the rhythm and movements that make you feel good and comfortable.
2. Then, visualize whatever's making you feel angry.
3. As your angry emotions feel stronger, up the intensity of your jumps. This will help you move through the emotions you're experiencing, gain some perspective, and clear your body of the bad feelings.
4. Finally, visualize yourself demolishing your anger by breaking through the image of whatever is causing it. The more energy and effort you invest, the more the emotional pain will be removed. (You can practice this for 20 minutes four times a week.)

Exercise #3: Yoga

Yoga involves a set of stress management techniques that bring you many physical and mental health benefits.[1] You can try different styles of yoga when you need some relief from anger in a constructive way. Even so, you don't need to be an expert to practice it, and the following basic poses are good places to start.

All yoga positions activate your parasympathetic nervous system, creating a sense of inward safety and concentration. They calm your mind while strengthening your body and enhancing your mind-body connection.

- *Corpse pose* (*savasana*). Lie down on your back on the floor (using a yoga mat for more comfort), keep your hands relaxed at your sides, and your feet slightly apart (with palms facing upward). You must get comfortable in the position, otherwise it'll be a painful experience. Now, focus on your breathing and stay in this position for five minutes.
- *Child's pose* (*balasana*). Kneel on the floor, sit back on your heels, and bend forward from your hips, making your chest touch your thighs. You can keep your hands extended in front of you or at your sides, touching the floor. Maintain this position for three to five minutes, and return to the original position.
- *Fish pose* (*matsyasana*). Sit in a *padmasana* or lotus pose. Hold your toes and lean back to stretch your spine and neck. Try to touch your head to the floor (your back should be arched),

but don't force yourself. Hold this position for a few seconds and then return to the lotus pose. The fish pose improves blood circulation to your head. If you don't know how to do the lotus pose, here are the instructions:

1. Sit on the floor with your knees bent, separated, and resting in a crossed position with your right leg on top.
2. Hold your right calf with both hands and rotate your shinbone away from you laterally. Then draw the right heel toward your navel, closing the knee.
3. Next, extend through your right foot in plantar flexion while your toes are pressing down. Put your right foot into the crease of the left hip, and reach through your right thigh bone, moving down the right knee.

- *Easy pose* (*sukhasana*). Start sitting on the floor with your legs crossed. Keep your back straight and your hands on your knees. Inhale deeply, focusing on your breathing, then slowly exhale; do this for five minutes. The easy pose also strengthens your back and improves your body posture.

- ***Shoulder stand pose*** (*sarvangasana*). Lying down on your back (with hands at your side and feet together), lift your legs up to form a 90-degree angle with your body. Next, support and lift your body further by bending your elbows and keeping your palms under your waist. Maintain this pose for five minutes and return to the original position. This pose improves body flexibility.

MEDITATION EXERCISES

Meditation mainly consists of teaching your mind to focus and guiding your nervous system to naturally balance itself. Meditation has scientifically proven effective in reducing negativity, stress, anger, and aggression. It's an excellent tool that helps awaken your consciousness and modifies your thoughts.[2]

When meditating, you quiet the amygdala's activity, shutting down your fight-or-flight response and reducing the production of damaging stress hormones such as cortisol. Hence, meditation exercises are an excellent strategy for you to address any physiological reactions to anger, fostering a sense of calm. They can disrupt your anger cycle and promote emotional self-regulation so that you can better interpret and respond to situations that make you mad.

Benefits of Meditation

- Concentrating on the present moment rather than a cycle of negative thoughts.
- Increasing your awareness of emotions and minimizing the tendency to react impulsively.
- Improving self-acceptance and your tolerance to cope with distress.
- Changing your mindset while releasing yourself from self-defeating negative thoughts.
- Strengthening your ability to observe what's happening without criticizing.

Exercise #1: Release Anger From the Body

This exercise focuses on the physical pain and tension you may experience. When you know the physical manifestation of anger, you can be aware of where you're holding it so that you can consciously release it. Here's how to do it:

1. As you breathe, start to focus on your feet; wiggle your toes, and flex and point your feet. Imagine the muscles of your feet letting go of anger.
2. Move your attention to your legs. Squeeze and then release the group of muscles in your legs. Try to imagine your legs letting the anger go.

3. Now focus on your torso. Inhale and visualize a cool, gentle wave flowing through your chest and abdomen, clearing your tension.

4. Next, address your attention to your neck and shoulders. Roll your shoulders a few times, lift them up to your ears, and slacken them. Then, move your neck, releasing the knots of anger.

5. Pay attention to your arms and hands as you tense and release the muscles in them. Curl your fingers into fists, then slacken. Now slowly shake them, visualizing the anger draining away.

6. Tune into the muscles of your face. Scrunch them and release them, allowing the tension to dissipate.

7. Now scan your whole body once more from head to toe. Check for any lingering tension, squeezing and releasing.

8. Picture your anger draining out of your body.

If you haven't practiced meditation before, here's some advice:

- Start meditating for five minutes a day, four times a week.
- Incorporate meditation into any of your routines (You can also combine meditation with the exercises explained in Chapter 6.)
- Find a peaceful spot without any distractions.
- Sit or lie down in a comfortable position.
- Notice your thoughts as you focus on one thing at a time (i.e., breathing, a sound, an image).
- Remove any expectations and judgments. Replace self-criticisms with gentle, forgiving thoughts.
- Be patient. Everything takes practice and time.

Exercise #2: Body Awareness

Body awareness refers to how connected your mind is to your body. It consists of being conscious of the position and movements of the body parts in relation to muscles and joints. When a person knows where their body is positioned in space, they can better direct it to do what they want, creating a sense of security.

Body awareness has excellent outcomes in health that involve better body balance and stability, weight and pain management, noticing personal feelings, meeting personal needs, and improving mental well-being. In this sense, some of the health outcomes of practicing body awareness are:

- higher self-esteem
- less depressive and anxiety symptoms
- vitality
- lower sensory pain
- stress relief
- better mood and sleep

Balance exercises involve simple physical activities, such as standing on one foot or walking in a straight line. Here are some other options:

- *Walking backward.* Believe it or not, this exercise forces you to connect to your body in a new way. It also activates muscles that you don't exercise regularly when walking. Before practicing, be sure to remove any obstacles from your path.
- *Body scan meditation.* It's a very helpful technique for scanning your whole body and becoming aware of sensations such as aches, pain, tension, and numbness. When you lean into these senses,

you learn to sit in the present and focus on every physical and emotional feeling. You aren't changing anything but are noticing everything, which is the first step to becoming present.

Exercise #3: Mindfulness Meditation

Managing anger in a healthier way involves self-reflection and using skills such as mindfulness meditation, self-compassion, and self-awareness.[3] Mindfulness meditation helps you evaluate your experiences without judgment or becoming overwhelmed. It teaches you that your thoughts, negative feelings, and physical responses are temporary, not who you are, which gives you increased freedom to choose how to react to them.

For instance, through mindfulness—acceptance of your moment-to-moment experience—you're in control of every situation. This awareness allows you to analyze the options available in responding to anger and the ability to differentiate between different emotions.

Furthermore, mindfulness improves your ability to respond constructively to relationship stress, conflict, and negativity. In addition, people with better mindfulness tend to experience less emotional stress when facing hostile relationships and enter conflicts with less anxiety and irritability.[4]

During this type of meditation, pay attention to what you notice, and practice letting things be for a while. I know it's hard, but with a little effort, you can achieve it. Here are the steps to help you master it:

1. Lie down or sit in a comfortable chair. If you decide to lie down, let your arms and legs fall to your sides. If you sit, do it in a balanced and stable position.
2. Take a few seconds to notice your breathing. Expect your mind to wander, and every time it happens, return your attention to your feet without fighting or criticizing yourself.

3. Now notice the pressure of your feet against the floor or bed, the temperature, comfort or discomfort, itches, pain, or any sensation. Keep your attention on your feet for a few minutes.

4. Then move the attention to your lower legs. You might feel the touch of clothing, the bed, or the chair, and you might feel nothing at all. Whatever you experience, that's what you're supposed to feel right now.

5. Wait a few minutes, and then shift the attention to your legs for a few minutes more.

6. Next, move to your abdomen and then to your chest. Focus on physical sensations like breathing, sounds in your stomach, and any manifestations of sadness, anger, tension, and so on.

7. Continue focusing on the other parts of your body, spending some minutes on each one: shoulders, hands, arms, and neck, releasing the tension you find in the process.

8. Finally, focus on your face and head. Notice any expressions of emotion around your eyes, forehead, and mouth.

9. Now pause before concluding. Take a moment of self-reflection and then decide when to move on with your day.

Once you're mindfully aware of your experiences, you become more sensitive to your suffering and see yourself as deserving of love and care. It embraces a healthy affirmation of oneself. Practicing self-compassion allows you to recognize anger as a signal of underlying pain that must be managed. Likewise, it helps you to judge your emotions less harshly, another way to mitigate anger.[5]

The next chapter will explore helpful exercises for the mind.

8

ANGER EXERCISES – THE MIND

Anger doesn't solve anything. It builds nothing, but it can destroy everything.

— LAWRENCE DOUGLAS WILDER

THOUGHT EXERCISES

Anger is linked to your thoughts. When you're angry, your thoughts and patterns become distorted, which destroys your ability to have a healthy life. Some forms of distorted thinking are taking things personally, ignoring the positive, blaming others, perfectionism, self-fulfilling prophecy (a tendency to draw negative conclusions about life), and black-and-white thinking (when life has also grays).

Self-awareness can lead you toward greater discipline to look at anger as it is—a natural emotion with advantages and setbacks. Hence, a shift in perspective can help you to prevent the adverse outcomes of distorted thinking patterns.

The following exercises will expand your mind. Remember that emotions are controlled more by thoughts than by external factors. However, they involve challenging activities, so keep trying and learning. Both optimal challenges and self-growth underlie happiness.

Exercise #1: Think Before You Speak

You've probably heard this phrase a hundred times, but it's important to remember it: Listening is a necessary aspect of the communication process, as it helps to identify with the speaker and enjoy experiences of empathy and belonging.[1] Active listening to what the other person says can prevent misunderstandings that otherwise could have led to big problems.

During a tense conversation, practice active listening by following some of these tips:

- Unplug from technology. Silent the mobile, for example.
- Observe changes in their tone.
- Focus on what they're saying.
- When you think the other person will stop talking, count to three in your mind. Then think about what's most important to say at the moment. You'll speak to create a connection.

- Try compassion by attempting to put yourself in the other person's shoes for a minute, even if you disagree, to try and see the issues from their perspective.
- Ask questions and show respect for opinions that are different from your own.
- Enjoy the process and practice understanding another person's viewpoint.

Exercise #2: Managing Your Thoughts

Arguing with yourself when contradictory thoughts are out of control is a natural response. Mind-wandering—characterized by a good deal of mental disagreement and disengagement—is a normal state. However, sometimes you need to be deeply focused on a mental task so that your mind enters into a state of flow in which thoughts, emotions, and actions are temporarily synchronized.

This exercise is for you to change your negative feelings rather than deny them; denial is unhealthy, as it steals valuable information that you can use to understand your anger. The first step is to accept that you're angry, and become aware of how complicated and intuitive your thinking process is. The following steps are explained below:

1. Acknowledge the presence of contradictory thoughts in your mind, even if it's uncomfortable. Think of your worries and anger as a movie playing in your mind. You'll begin to feel calmer while easing the emotions and physical sensations that arise when you're mad.
2. As you listen to your thoughts, notice when your mind starts to chatter. Then take a minute to point them in any direction.
3. Next, distinguish between solvable and unsolvable problems and track them as they continue running through your mind.
4. Write down everything you notice. You can keep an anger diary, and make it a goal to write down every negative feeling and thought you have when angry.
5. After completing this exercise, repeat it two more times, letting your thoughts run for one minute each time.
6. In the second round, determine whether each thought is appropriate. At this point, their loudness may have increased; try to focus more on their meaning.
7. In the third round, adopt a posture of curiosity and amusement while listening to your noisy thoughts. Here, the specific content of them

seems less important, so instead take a step back from them.

With this exercise, you're training your mind to be calmer and less reactive. However, be careful if you feel a sense of freedom and distance in the minutes after practicing these exercises; your mind might try to convince you that your problems are solved, which isn't the truth.

Another helpful technique to control your thoughts is to practice being present through mindfulness meditation. This means focusing on one thing—without distraction or wanting to be somewhere else—and letting yourself feel whatever emotion you feel, even challenging ones.

The benefits of managing your thoughts go beyond productivity and goals. This exercise helps you trust yourself, spend quality time with your loved ones, and find joy in every experience. When you're able to do this, you'll be at ease with both difficulty and joy, comfort and discomfort.

Other ways to be more present include:

- body scan or body awareness
- mindful eating (Engage all the senses when you eat, and take time to savor each component of your meal.)
- pausing screen time for a while
- building a routine

KNOWING EXERCISES

Exercise #1: Identifying Your Anger Triggers

From the beginning of this book, I've emphasized understanding your anger and identifying what causes it. For example, things like:

- being treated unfairly
- experiencing dishonesty or disappointment
- being under pressure and frustration
- encountering threats to self-esteem
- facing prejudice and discrimination
- getting physically attacked
- suffering depression or anxiety

This is a key exercise in anger management, and you can practice it by identifying the reason why you're angry (situations, people, thoughts, etc.), taking a step back, and defining your sense of unfairness (from a moral and emotional perspective). As a result, you'll better understand your sticking points and emotional catalysts.

Exercise #2: Learn to Problem-Solve

Learning problem-solving techniques is a must, not only for your work, but also your daily life. It requires a systematic step-by-step approach. Take a look at some basic stages you can follow when approaching any issue:

1. ***Identify the problem.*** It seems an easy task, but involves more than willingness. It will help if you analyze all the aspects that the issue embraces.
2. ***Do your research.*** As you do in any college project or at the office, once you know the problem and define it, find its nature and its triggers.
3. ***Find possible solutions.*** This stage requires you to be creative. Brainstorming is an excellent start to come up with potential solutions. Be sure to think of different solutions so that you have plans A, B, C, and even D.

4. ***Make a decision.*** To make a decision, narrow down your list to the best solutions possible. Don't hurry at this stage.

5. ***Implement the solution with an accurate plan.*** If it doesn't work, remember you have a back-up plan.

6. ***Follow up with your solution.*** Observe if the solution is working and decide if other actions or adjustments are necessary.

CALMING EXERCISES

Exercise #1: Taking a Time-out

This is a classic anger management tool, but a challenging one. It involves removing yourself from a triggering situation so that you have time to calm down and gain a clearer outlook. It's a healthy way to manage anger before it gets out of control.

When emotions are getting more intense, communication becomes less clear and healthy. Therefore, taking time to calm oneself sets the basis to conduct a more productive dialogue or perform well-controlled actions.

A time-out can occur on an informal level, where you simply take a break from an overwhelming situation. For example, instead of answering a call in an angry manner, you can take a time-out and return the call after you've cooled off.

How to practice this technique:

1. Identify ways to take a time-out, such as going to another room, going for a walk, or just sitting and being silent for a while. You should think of different options in advance, because when anger rises, you won't be thinking clearly.
2. You should inform others at home or at the office that you may use this resource and explain to them its purpose to avoid any confusion about your actions.
3. Follow up on your anger levels to prevent yourself from hitting the boiling point. The objective is to notice when you're about to engage in any destructive and hostile behaviors.
4. Next, take the time-out. Implement the ways you chose to calm yourself and let go of whatever caused your anger.
5. Finally, when you return from the time-out, if you've calmed considerably, then go ahead with some problem-solving strategies. If you still need more time, take it until you're ready to re-engage in an activity.

Exercise #2: Talk to a Buddy

Anger management also involves the support of your loved ones. When you're experiencing a severe episode of anger, you may try to call a close friend, especially if your safety is in danger. Think of the people that will be with you in hard times, and don't hesitate to ask them for help when you feel overwhelmed. A hug, a smile, or even hearing "I'm here" can bring peace to your mind and heal you.

Talking to someone else about your feelings can be very hard. At a young age, I used to be a very introverted person; my family and friends didn't have any clue about my feelings and behaviors. Once I realized how much sharing my feelings could help, I started to see a lot of improvement in my communication skills and daily well-being.

Of course, this process requires us to be brave and vulnerable, but it's necessary to make progress in our mental health journey. I know it's scary, considering you can't always trust everyone, especially to communicate your fears and show your more vulnerable side. But every time you open yourself up instead of closing off, you open a door for a healthier path and take a step further towards a solution.

Exercise #3: The Calming Kit

The "calming kit" is inspired by young children who experience intense emotions, but lack the vocabulary and self-regulation skills to control them effectively. The kit includes a series of tools and strategies to understand complex feelings, ask for help, and learn to manage emotions. Even though it has primarily been designed for children, anyone can benefit from it.

The calming kit includes items such as:

- bubble wrap
- a soft blanket
- a massager
- stress balls
- an eye mask
- a pressure vest
- puzzles, crosswords, etc.

- affirmation cards (You can create your own or purchase them.)
- blank notepads
- books or audiobooks
- nature sounds
- balance cushion
- essential oils
- an hourglass
- scented candles
- a deep breathing printout
- yoga cards
- chewing gum
- a punching bag
- a jump rope
- resistance bands
- an exercise ball
- calm-down bottles
- a lava lamp
- a photo album

In the next chapter, we'll move on to some exercises for anger management that address families, partners, and children.

9

ANGER EXERCISES – THE FAMILY

Always remember when it comes to family arguments and disputes, blood is thicker than anger.

— STANLEY VICTOR PASKAVICH

You may have inherited unhealthy coping anger mechanisms from your parents and/or grandparents and passed them on from generation to generation. However, you can work on this as a family and interrupt the cycle.

Although some experts affirm anger is a genetic condition, most agree that anger is a learned behavior when it isn't triggered by any mental health issue. The family members teach children how to express their feelings. If the family doesn't manage anger appropriately, the kids are likely to exhibit the same behaviors. It depends on each of them to decide if their behaviors are helping or hurting the family and take action about it.

If you feel that you're passing anger on to your children, first remember that you're the role model, and that anger is never the primary feeling. It's essential to encourage a family environment where everyone can talk freely about their emotions without judgment. If you can handle your anger, you'll break the chain that's being passed along through generations, and open the door towards happiness.

FAMILY ENVIRONMENT EXERCISES

Exercise #1: The Safe Space

Having a safe place, physically or virtually, for when you need to open up and ask for help is the key to mental health. Such a place provides you with an environment where you feel loved and confident instead of regretful, defensive, or afraid. When you feel optimistic and calm, you can work towards changing more freely.

Let's explore some tips to make every space a safe space:

- Make room for who you are, including the elements (mental or physical) that make you feel happy.
- Build a culture of trust that is forgiving and welcomes openness.

- Be vulnerable and allow yourself to build an emotional connection with others. This will open your mind and soul to new people and experiences.
- Be inclusive and open to diversity.
- Give people included in this space the chance to talk. Remember active listening.
- Offer honesty and accountability by showing others how welcomed they are in your space and how their well-being is a priority for you.
- If it's a physical environment, make it a welcoming and comfortable space, where everyone can feel relaxed and open to sharing their emotions.

Exercise #2: The Anger Iceberg

The anger iceberg embraces the idea that anger is the tip of the iceberg, and other emotions are hidden beneath the surface. These other feelings (i.e., sadness, fear, loneliness, insecurity, pain, guilt, anxiety, frustration, grief, shame, stress, etc.) may cause you to feel more vulnerable and hopeless.

Once you've identified the triggers of your anger, get to the root of the deeper emotion and prioritize that over your anger. For example, if it's fear, work on what you're afraid of; if it's guilt, you may need to focus on the actions you performed that made you feel that way.

Therefore, start thinking of anger like an iceberg to understand its essence. By exploring what's beneath the surface, you can gain insight into your anger, such as solutions and strategies to cope with it.

Exercise #3: The Empathy

Empathy is seeing a situation from others' perspectives, considering their history, values, needs, personality, and dreams. In marriage, empathy is putting yourself in your partner's shoes as they vent, considering all the variables that make them who they are. But how can you become more empathetic with your spouse and other family members? Dr. Wyatt Fisher has some suggestions[1]:

1. "Two birds on the same branch." The concept was created by John Gottman, an American psychologist who's an expert in marriage research. When your spouse is venting, imagine they're on their branch looking at the issue from their perspective, while you see the issue from the opposite branch (a different angle). Consequently, you question their viewpoint and even criticize it. You reject their viewpoint or oppose them because you're looking at the

issue from your branch, which causes severe problems in the relationship. Therefore, you should try to move on and fly to their branch to see the topic from their view, which means that empathy isn't trying to see something from your perspective and only resonating with your partner. It's to kick off your shoes and put on their shoes, remembering who they are. Then, it will make sense why the issue made them feel bad.

2. In the family environment, take turns asking one another questions like, "What was most challenging for you growing up?" "What are your core values?" "What are your main fears and insecurities?" "What do you like the most?" "What makes you worry the most?" "What makes you feel calm or at peace?" "What are your top needs and priorities?" "What are your plans for the future?" Such questions will provide all of you with rich information on who your family members and partners are, why they behave in that way, and how they see and experience the world. Take note of the answers and review them often.

3. Another key aspect of empathy is to avoid giving any advice in response to your family venting unless they ask you for it. When you

give them advice without being asked, it will make them feel frustrated and unheard.

EXERCISES FOR DEALING WITH YOUR PARTNER'S ANGER

Exercise #1: The Angry Partner

We discussed in Chapter 3 that an angry partner's hostile attitude and behaviors can drain others' energy and leave them frustrated, and it can undermine the health of the partnership. However, if you can deal with an angry partner, your relationship will transform into a positive nexus. Among the most effective strategies to deal with an angry partner are:

- ***De-escalate and neutralize the emotions.*** Avoid getting mad in response to your partner's anger. Don't confront them if they behave aggressively. Instead, let them be angry. The calmer you remain, the quicker they calm down.

- ***Give them time to calm down.*** When you notice that the conversation isn't taking either of you anywhere—instead, it's making things worse—give them space to cool off and notice their behavior. You can sleep in another room or spend a few days apart.

- ***Be assertive and respectful.*** Pay more attention to the way you speak when making them notice they're acting in a wrong way. If you hear yourself talking too loud or rapidly, adjust your speech accordingly. Acting assertively is a position in which you can express your wants directly while also considering your partner's feelings, opinions, and wants. In the same way, your partner may take their part of the responsibility for the issue. Learning to be assertive can be challenging, but you can try to:

  - think about the outcome you want to achieve
  - be specific

◦ carefully listen to their words and try to understand their point of view

◦ expect the conversation to go wrong and spot it when it's happening

- ***Validate and understand.*** Validation is when you communicate acceptance of yourself and others, but it doesn't mean agreeing with everything. The key is to consider their perspective, be present, and be beneath the surface to understand their deepest feelings.
- ***Be patient and kind.*** Avoid blaming and accusing them. Instead, use patience as an antidote to their anger, which means being wise at the moment anger arises. It's about waiting before acting or speaking.
- ***Be responsible.*** Being responsible in this context is to accept your role in being frustrated with an angry partner and reflect on not only what actions may trigger their anger, but also what triggers you to react to their anger. The more conscious you become, the more constructive and optimistic you'll be.
- ***Help them identify their triggers.*** Try this when you're both feeling calm, away from any conflict or bad situation. Recognizing the triggers for anger helps you both plan how to

manage it and how to communicate when it arises. Help them seek professional advice if necessary.

- ***Discuss the issue when your partner is calm.*** Only when both of you are calm, start discussing the problem that led to your spouse's angry outburst. By doing this, you may help them to be willing to listen to your words and assimilate to them. Also, don't forget to apply this rule to yourself.

- ***Do not try to change your partner.*** When having problems in your marriage, influence, not change, your partner's perspective, and show them the benefits of your position. You can influence them by creating a positive atmosphere where cooperation, support, love, and empathy are the core values. When you treat your spouse with sweetness and respect, you may bring them closer to you. Use kind and motivational words during the process.

- ***Set boundaries.*** In your relationship, be clear in advance about what behavior is and isn't permissible for you, and think about what action you can take if they cross the limit. You don't have to deal with any behavior that causes you pain or suffering and makes you feel unsafe.

- ***Consider the situation as an opportunity to learn.*** You both often need to step back, look at each other, and concentrate on the best of each other, creating a greater sense of intimacy.
- ***Seek win-win solutions.*** Find a solution to family anger that leaves both of you feeling that you got something valuable from it.

Exercise #2: Practicing Forgiveness

Forgiveness is considered one of the most effective strategies to reduce and master anger in marriage. It's awful when the person you love the most hurts you, as it lowers your ability to trust and weakens your confidence. Still, there's always space for forgiveness. It involves uncovering anger from your marriage and deciding to work on letting go of that anger without misdirecting it at children or others.

Forgiveness therapy is a psychologically proven method that helps in diminishing and resolving the damage caused by explosive anger.[2] For instance, it can help you forget past bad experiences, facilitate reconciliation, and decrease the likelihood that anger will disrupt the relationship. Some studies have also demonstrated that forgiveness improves self-confidence and helps address the symptoms of sadness and anxiety, and eventually prevents the recurrence of these feelings.[3]

Although forgiveness is the simplest method to manage anger, it doesn't come naturally. Here's how you can practice forgiveness in two key steps:

1. You and your partner need to identify your childhood experiences of being hurt or disappointed by parents or others.
2. Both have to try to understand the other side's parental relationships. As this task proceeds, you develop the awareness that a spouse's behaviors can most often be attributed to past emotional hurts from family members. This is basically to look at the past to understand the present when either of you deliberately inflicts hurt on the other.

Exercise #3: Controlling Relationship Anger

- *Avoid the impulse to react aggressively.* When feeling too angry, tell your partner that you need some time to cool off so you can organize your thoughts.
- *Focus on managing yourself.* Remember you cannot control anyone's thoughts, actions, or emotions, you can only control yourself. Being

calm is much more mature and effective than trying to calm the other person, and gives them the space to do the same.

- *Be aware of triangles.* Sometimes, when you use a third person to manage your anger about your spouse, such action keeps you from working out the problem in the relationship. It can make your partner feel isolated or react in a defensive and hostile manner. If your purpose is to ask for someone's help to be on your side and agree with you, it's better to try calming yourself down first before calling someone else. There's nothing wrong with sharing your conflicts with a friend, an expert, or a relative, but make them understand that their job is to be objective, without taking sides, and help you think of a good solution.
- *Analyze past issues.* Analyze previous situations that triggered similar episodes to detect a pattern and find the best solution.
- *A relationship is 50/50.* Each person should invest the same amount of energy, time, and effort into their relationship. If you're calmer and more mature during an argument, then your relationship becomes more mature. Maybe they'll rise to the same level of maturity, or you'll realize that the relationship isn't

healthy or suitable for you. Either way, you're already doing the correct thing by controlling your emotions and choosing not to let anger overpower you.

DEALING WITH CHILDREN'S ANGER EXERCISES

Children who experience stress, frustration, anxiety, and anger episodes have problems building social relationships, interacting positively with others, and being open to learning and curiosity (both essential aspects during childhood).

When children are unsure how to handle their feelings, frustration and anger quickly transform into disrespect, disobedience, aggression, and tantrums. There are different ways to teach kids how to handle their anger. Now, we'll discuss some of them.

Exercise #1: The Angry Child

Anger is also a common and natural emotion in children, but they manage it differently from us. Anger is the traditional channel through which both children and teens tell you "I need help!" or "I need something!" The louder the cry, the more urgent the need. Likewise, the fact that teen years involve significant hormonal changes further complicates the experience of emotions. Therefore, learning to manage angry children and teens is an ongoing process that requires specific techniques and strategies. Here are some of them:

- Don't yell at them or challenge them during an angry outburst. If you yell at them and lose control, it'll worsen the situation and make them engage in a power struggle.
- Don't try to reason with them. Reasoning with an angry kid or teen is always a challenge, because they don't have the same capacity to reflect as adults do. Wait until they calm down and discuss it later.
- Watch out for your feelings and responses. If you also become angry, try to calm yourself before you help your child. Use self-talk and take several deep breaths. Children tend to copy our actions, so try to stay calm, and they may respond positively. Try role models for dealing with your negative emotions as a lesson for them.
- Don't get physical when dealing with angry children or teenagers. This can make the situation escalate, and you're teaching them to solve problems with aggression.
- Get them to a safe environment. Most kids destroy the things around them when angry. If you're not in a secure spot when your child is experiencing such emotions, remove any harmful items around, and try to get them to a safe place.

- Take a different approach with younger kids (from four to fifteen years old). If your child is in the midst of a tantrum, you can move slightly away from them, but without isolating them. Help them learn that they can have a role in calming themselves down; thus, let them cool off until they feel in control. By doing so, you're asking them to pay attention to themselves.

- After the anger episode, talk to them. When speaking, make sure you use a neutral, calm, and soft tone. Be specific, keep it short, and repeat the exact phrase every time you can. At that age, repeating is helpful because they still have difficulty processing information. Use reinforcing phrases like "I'm here for you," "I love you," "I want to help you," and "I understand."

- Give them consequences for their actions, not for their emotions. When your kid throws a tantrum or starts screaming, make sure you give them consequences according to such actions, but don't punish them severely. When you just focus on punishing them, you're actually forcing them to stop by force. This action will make them behave worse, keeping the same wrong behavior.

Exercise #2: The Calm-Down Box

A calm-down box is an excellent and entertaining tool to help your children or yourself regulate mind and body so you all can build resilience and cope during the most stressful circumstances. A calm down box contains your child's favorite items to help them self-regulate, regain a regular heart rate, and center themselves. Such boxes are focused on sensory exercises for feeling, smelling, hearing, and practicing deep breathing.

The main steps to design a calm-down box are explained below:

- Make sure your child likes what's inside and that all items are age-appropriate:

  - Some calm-down box ideas for toddlers may include sensory/activity books, crayons, stickers, coloring pages, toys, flashcards that visually depict biological needs/emotions, pinwheels, etc. Ideas for children's calm-down boxes include legos, slime, kinetic sand, books, art supplies, colorful cards, dolls, cars, or any other items that encourage them to play by themselves and act out emotions.

- ○ Don't include screen time with the calm-down box (i.e., video games, electronic devices, etc.).

- Write little notes around to jog your memory about the calm-down box or schedule time in your day to practice.
- Model the calm-down box and show your child how to use it. You can practice together.
- Encourage your child to use their box independently. A calm-down box is designed to encourage self-regulation and independent play.
- Make them understand that feelings aren't bad, but there are healthy ways to manage them, like a calm-down box.
- Always put the box in the same place so it's easy for them to find it.
- As your child grows, you have to help them adapt the content of their calm-down box as their interests change over time.

Exercise #3: Coping Skills

Coping is a skill that every child has to learn, and parents can be a huge help to them when it comes to teaching such a skill.

You can help them choose from several strategies that work, such as:

- distracting themselves (shifting their focus onto something more positive)
- creating some distance from the angry situation (walking or playing)
- relaxing away from the tension they feel (taking deep breaths)
- remembering something funny
- using their imagination to find a safe place in their minds to be away from anger
- asking for help when facing a problem
- reading books about anger. Children's books that cover anger are great teaching aids. They usually contain lessons about how to manage anger.

In addition, children and teens can manage their anger with simple techniques, such as:

- shredding paper
- drinking cold water
- taking a break
- using pop bubble wrap
- playing with playdough

- wrapping their arms around themself and squeezing
- jumping on a trampoline
- writing down what's bothering them and crumpling it up
- squeezing a stress ball
- talking about it
- doing jumping jacks
- putting the palms together, pushing, and then relaxing

Along with these basic strategies, as a parent, you need to:

- ***Identify triggers.*** Start by asking them about what makes them worried or angry. Help them identify those factors so you can both use the information for the next time. The anger iceberg technique can be helpful here.
- ***Help them identify where they feel anger in their bodies.*** Sometimes, kids don't know they're angry until after the anger runs out. Help them notice the signs their body gives them when feeling mad. Over time, they'll start to recognize the emotion and use coping skills before things get too overwhelming.

- *Use a feelings thermometer* to help children make the connection between their feelings and their coping skills:

  - Tell them to pick three colors, one for each section of the thermometer, and color it in.
  - Then, talk about each section: Ask them what it looks like when they're a little angry at the bottom of the thermometer. Next, move on to the middle section; if they're medium-sized angry, what does it look like? Finally, at the top of the thermometer, talk about how it looks when they're experiencing deep anger.

- *Identify the coping skill that your child would like to try.* Take a few minutes three times a week to work with them on this and encourage them to practice a coping skill they would use next time they feel angry. Make sure they have all mechanisms that will help them at each level of anger, alongside different options for each level, because remember that not all coping skills work in specific situations.

Teaching your child to vent their anger by shouting or hitting something might provide temporary relief. Eventually, it will cause more anger and increased aggressive behavior; it's like a snowball. Therefore, they need to learn to manage their anger through coping skills to deal with negative feelings. Yet, remember that anger management is a process. Little by little, they'll get better at it with practice and discipline. Encourage them to work on it and be responsible for their actions.

There you have it! With these exercises, you'll have a better hold on your and your family's emotions, and will be able to keep your anger from harming your relationships again.

Just don't forget to reward yourself every time you complete an exercise. When you positively affirm yourself, you'll make a habit out of productive self-care.

CONCLUSION

Anger consists of powerful social emotion, and it's better to approach it as a set of processes, including the triggers, development, management, expression, and outcomes. Even though feeling angry is a natural part of life, it isn't an emotion that everybody really feels comfortable with, perhaps because some of them haven't been taught the skills to effectively handle it.

It's okay to feel angry. Anger can help get you through complicated feelings and situations and motivate you to change the things in your life that make you frustrated or unhappy. This motivating force helps you enhance communications in both personal and professional relationships, and contributes to optimism, among other benefits.

Altruism is often born out of anger; no emotion is stronger when mobilizing others and building support for a cause. Unlike fear and sadness, anger provides a burst of energy, making us feel powerful and in command instead of vulnerable and powerless. If things don't go as they should and need to be changed, anger empowers you to do something about it. It eventually motivates you to find the right solutions to any of your problems.

If you've ever felt the urge to take action following an angry outburst, you've experienced this human emotion's positive side. After experiencing an anger outburst, this impulse for action may be beneficial and productive in helping you decide what's most important to you, identify the changes your life needs, and determine how to move forward into a happy life.

Consequently, anger can be a positive emotion, so long as you use it to resolve problems and acknowledge conflicts. Keeping your anger expressions grounded in reason and your responses to anger proportionate is the key to channeling the positive side of anger. It's essential that you embrace anger as a normal emotion and, rather than acting upon it negatively, learn how to channel it in a healthier manner so that you don't carry it around like a heavy weight.

Anger can decrease violence, be beneficial to relationships, foster optimism, and be a helpful, motivating force, but it can also easily be disruptive. Anger, as a powerful emotion, can be expressed indirectly and negatively when it isn't recognized. When not handled properly, it can lead to devastating outcomes for yourself and the people closest to you.

Chronic anger takes from your large amounts of mental energy, making it difficult to focus on the positive things. Even if your anger is warranted, you can feel better about yourself by picking your most important fights and leaving the rest behind. When you ignore, dismiss, or even mock your thoughts and feelings, it may lead to feelings of unfairness, shame, and self-loathing.

Bottled-up anger is more likely to trigger an abrupt, intense explosion when least expected. Instead, think of anger as coming in fast and slow varieties, where you want to yell and where you want to motivate someone with calculated means. It can be misused, both at work and in personal relationships, by dominating and intimidating others.

In addition, keeping anger in may lead to passive-aggressive behaviors, being critical, and being hostile to others. In the same way, repressing your anger without addressing the mistreatment does nothing to rectify the situation, and can result in diminished self-esteem.

Overall, angry feelings may also lead you to turn away from the world and take the anger inward, affecting your health and well-being. Failing to control it may cause various problems, such as saying things you regret, screaming at your children, threatening co-workers, sending unkind emails, developing mental health issues, or even resorting to physical violence. In this sense, anger becomes problematic when it's often felt with too much intensity, which can have physical, mental, and social costs.

For instance, higher anger traits, chronic hostility, and angry expression may result in cardiovascular diseases. Compared with sadness, anger increases the risk of chronic illness in adults, and scientific research supports this. Constantly operating under high levels of stress and anger makes you more vulnerable not only to heart disease, but also to diabetes, a compromised immune system, insomnia, hypertension, respiratory problems, and chronic depression.

The key is learning how to handle anger just as with any other emotion, and to channel it into the right actions. Learning how to manage anger is to minimize the negative consequences of this powerful emotion while maximizing the positive ones. Even so, the real purpose of anger management isn't to repress feelings of anger, but to understand the message behind emotion and express it positively without losing control. Therefore, anger management involves several skills that assist you with recognizing the signs of anger and positively dealing with triggers.

An essential step towards managing your anger is to recognize that you experience anger outbursts and make a step forward to improve. If you fail to do so, anger management becomes ineffective. No matter how strong the experience of anger is, acting on that emotion without acknowledging why it's there can feel good for a moment, but it often causes you to act in ways that you later regret, and rarely helps address the root problem causing the anger.

Henceforth, when you recognize the anger triggers, you can act in advance so that the anger doesn't escalate too much. Similarly, being aware of the alerting signs when you're about to lose your temper will allow you to control your anger on time. When we're mindful that we're feeling anger, we can use that to inform our next actions, with the energy/anger being our motivation. If you view anger as something that makes you more aware, you can adjust your responses accordingly to improve your situation.

On the other hand, building habits that encourage you to experience more positive emotions may help you feel happier, perform better, and decrease negative feelings. Unjustified anger—or any other negative feeling—doesn't have to control you, and as you've learned in this book, there are many ways you can still feel it without letting it take over. Stressful events are no excuse for anger, but understanding how those events influence you can help you control the circumstances around you and avoid needless aggravation.

If you believe that an issue is worth getting angry about and that there's a possibility to improve the situation, then you should try to express your feelings in a healthy manner. Remind yourself that getting angry won't solve anything; it won't make you feel better (and may make you feel worse). Give yourself a reminder every time you feel that anger is getting the best of you to help you to obtain a more balanced outlook.

The exercises and techniques explained in this book can help you with it. With these tools to control your temper, you and your family can learn how to vent emotions without hurting each other, and prevent your mood from taking over your life. Of course, different techniques are effective for different people, but finding one method that works for you may be key in reversing episodes of extreme anger.

If you work to identify your anger and then manage it, it won't have as destructive an impact on your relationships, body, mind, and emotions. What you do with this anger matters, which is why grown-ups should study anger cues and strategies for keeping the way they react to situations positive and productive.

Evaluate whether your anger is medium-to-intense, experienced often, sustained to the point that you're holding grudges and planning on getting even, and expressed through aggressive verbal and physical actions. You must pay attention to signs like rage, irritability, chest tightness, increased energy, heart palpitations, tremors, racing thoughts, an increasing sense of tension, and poor communication. If you're inclined to turn to rage, you're probably at risk of having adverse relationships, health, and sometimes legal consequences of expressing your anger inappropriately.

In this case, you must start to address it through coping anger mechanisms. If your anger is still getting out of hand despite practicing anger management exercises, you should seek help from a mental health counselor. Likewise, when your partner or children are struggling to control their anger, don't hesitate to ask for professional help. In such cases, a therapist or mental health professional will aid you in addressing the underlying factors contributing to anger and other emotional problems.

Explaining the above, building a healthy life and happy home is a significant endeavor, and those who prioritize them reap tremendous rewards. We all want a healthier, happier life, without stress or anger controlling us. This is possible by working with your loved ones hand-in-hand; families stick close together and help one another out during the ups and downs of life.

Figure out different methods to better communicate your emotions to your children in ways they receive well, and accept blame when you make parenting mistakes. It can dramatically increase the bonds in the family and help you raise happier, more grateful children instead of entitled ones. Remember, every family is different, so you might have to tailor the steps above to fit your own life and needs, but doing it this way will benefit you and everyone in your family.

Life is incredibly stressful nowadays, and uncertainty is often one of the most difficult things to deal with in modern times. But accepting uncertainty and leaning into your fear of the unknown can make a difference in your overall well-being. So when embarking on your quest to create a happier, more positive life, keep in mind this isn't an elaborate process. It takes hard work, commitment, and dedication, but it's well worth it.

If you made it to this point, CONGRATULATIONS! Now that you have a comprehensive overview of anger management and have learned the basic coping mechanisms, you can start working on yourself and make a difference in your life.

I hope you've enjoyed reading this book just as I've enjoyed writing it.

If you found the information helpful to improve your anger management skills, please take a moment to leave a review of the book.

Thank you!

NOTES

INTRODUCTION

1. (Schieman, 2006).
2. (Stevens, 2010).

1. THE ANGER ENCYCLOPEDIA

1. (American Psychological Association, 2012).
2. (Schieman, 2006).
3. (Alia-Klein et al., 2020).
4. (Doyle Gentry, 2007).
5. (Alia-Klein et al., 2020).
6. (Scott, 2021).
7. (Doyle Gentry, 2007).
8. (American Psychological Association, 2012).
9. (Rothenberg, 1971).
10. (American Psychological Association, 2012).
11. (Lerner & Keltner, 2001).
12. (Aarts et al., 2010).
13. (American Psychological Association, 2012).
14. (American Psychological Association, 2012).
15. (Schwartz, n.d.).
16. (Schwartz, n.d.).

2. IDENTIFYING YOUR ANGER

1. (Cowlishaw et al., 2020).
2. (Schieman, 2006).

3. THE RIGHTS AND WRONGS OF ANGER

1. (Seladi-Schulman, 2018).
2. (Hendricks et al., 2013).
3. (Hendricks et al., 2013).
4. (Devlin, 2019).
5. (Schieman, 2006).
6. (Hendricks et al., 2013).
7. (Hendricks et al., 2013).
8. (Devlin, 2019).
9. (Baas cited in Manning-Schaffel, 2017).
10. (Wilson as cited in Manning-Schaffel, 2017).
11. (Devlin, 2019).
12. (Hendricks et al., 2013).
13. (APA, 2012; Ohwovoriole, 2021).
14. (Alia-Klein et al., 2020).
15. (Cowlishaw et al., 2020; Hendricks et al., 2013; Staicu & Cutov, 2010).
16. (Stevens, 2010).
17. (Aiken as cited in Strong, 2015).
18. (Chida & Steptoe, 2009).
19. (Strong, 2015).
20. (Strong, 2015).
21. (Alia-Klein et al., 2020).
22. (Cowlishaw et al., 2020).
23. (Strong, 2015).
24. (Wilson as cited in Manning-Schaffel, 2017).
25. (Schieman, 2006; Staicu & Cutov, 2010).
26. (Strong, 2015).
27. (Cowlishaw et al., 2020; Staicu & Cutov, 2010).
28. (Barlow et al., 2019).
29. (Doyle Gentry, 2007).
30. (Doyle Gentry, 2007).
31. (Schieman, 2006).
32. (Schieman, 2006).

33. (Doyle Gentry, 2007).
34. (Schieman, 2006).

4. ANGER IN ALL ITS FORMS

1. (Sukhodolsky et al., 2016).
2. (Sukhodolsky et al., 2016).
3. (Schieman, 2006).

5. BOTTLING UP AND ERUPTIONS

1. (Mullen as cited in Rose, 2021).
2. (Moore as cited in Lindberg, 2019).
3. (Moore as cited in Lindberg, 2019).
4. (Mullen as cited in Rose, 2021).
5. (Hammond, 2014).
6. (Hammond, 2014).
7. (Parrott & Giancola, 2007).
8. (Cleveland Clinic, 2022).
9. (Cleveland Clinic, 2022).
10. (Mayo Clinic, 2018).
11. (Cleveland Clinic, 2022).
12. (Cleveland Clinic, 2022).
13. (Mayo Clinic, 2018).
14. (Mayo Clinic, 2018).
15. (APA, n.d.).

6. ANGER EXERCISES – RELAXATION

1. (Brennan, 2021).
2. (Brennan, 2021).
3. (Clark, 2020).
4. (Nunez, 2020).

7. ANGER EXERCISES – THE BODY

1. (Granath et al., 2006).
2. (Gupta et al., 2015).
3. (Golden, 2016).
4. (Golden, 2016).
5. (Golden, 2016).

8. ANGER EXERCISES – THE MIND

1. (Raymond as cited in How to (really) think before you speak, 2021).

9. ANGER EXERCISES – THE FAMILY

1. (Fisher, n.d.).
2. (Fitzgibbons, 2019).
3. (Enright as cited in Fitzgibbons, 2019).

BIBLIOGRAPHY

Aarts, H., Ruys, K. I., Veling, H., Renes, R. A., de Groot, J. H. B., van Nunen, A. M., & Geertjes, S. (2010). The art of anger: Reward context turns avoidance responses to anger-related objects into approach. *Psychological Science, 21*(10), 1406–1410.

Alia-Klein, N., Gan, G., Gilam, G., Bezek, J., Bruno, A., Denson, T. F., Hendler, T., Lowe, L., Mariotti, V., Muscatello, M. R., Palumbo, S., Pellegrini, S., Pietrini, P., Rizzo, A., & Verona, E. (2020). The feeling of anger: From brain networks to linguistic expressions. *Neuroscience & Biobehavioral Reviews, 108*, 480-497.

American Psychological Association. (2011). *Strategies for controlling your anger: Keeping anger in check.* APA. https://www.apa.org/topics/anger/strategies-controlling

American Psychological Association. (2012). *How to recognize and deal with anger.* APA. https://www.apa.org/topics/anger/recognize

A quote by Ali Ibn Abu Talib. (n.d.). Goodreads. https://www.goodreads.com/quotes/7177814-a-moment-of-patience-in-a-moment-of-anger-saves

A quote by Ambrose Bierce. (n.d.). Goodreads. https://www.goodreads.com/quotes/9909-speak-when-you-are-angry-and-you-will-make-the

A quote from White Night. (n.d.). Goodreads. https://www.goodreads.com/quotes/214421-anger-is-just-anger-it-isn-t-good-it-isn-t-bad

Arun Gandhi quotes (Author of The gift of anger). (n.d.). Goodreads. https://www.goodreads.com/author/quotes/172354.Arun_Gandhi

Barlow, M. A., Wrosch, C., Gouin, J.-P., & Kunzmann, U. (2019). Is anger, but not sadness, associated with chronic inflammation and illness in older adulthood? *Psychology and Aging, 34*(3), 330–340.

Brennan, D. (2021, October 25). *What to know about alternate-nostril breathing.* WebMD. https://www.webmd.com/balance/what-to-know-about-alternate-nostril-breathing

Cherry, K. (2019, September 18). *How to understand and identify passive-aggressive behavior.* Verywell Mind. https://www.verywellmind.com/what-is-passive-aggressive-behavior-2795481

Chida, Y., & Steptoe, A. (2009). The association of anger and hostility with future coronary heart disease. *Journal of the American College of Cardiology, 53*(11), 936–946.

Clark, S. (2020, April 9). *How coherent breathing can help your anxiety.* Verywell Mind. https://www.verywellmind.com/an-overview-of-coherent-breathing-4178943

Cleveland Clinic. (2022, May 20). *Intermittent explosive disorder.* Cleveland Clinic. https://my.clevelandclinic.org/health/diseases/17786-intermittent-explosive-disorder

Cowlishaw, S., Metcalf, O., Varker, T., Stone, C., Molyneaux, R., Gibbs, L., Block, K., Harms, L., MacDougall, C., Gallagher, H. C., Bryant, R., Lawrence-Wood, E., Kellett, C., O'Donnell, M., & Forbes, D. (2020). Anger dimensions and mental health following a disaster: Distribution and implications after a major bushfire. *Journal of Traumatic Stress, 34*(1), pp.46-55.

Devlin, H. (2019, May 12). *Science of anger: how gender, age and personality shape this emotion.* The Guardian; The Guardian. https://www.theguardian.com/lifeandstyle/2019/may/12/science-of-anger-gender-age-personality

Doyle Gentry, W. (2007). *Anger management for dummies.* Wiley Pub., Inc.

Elliott, C. H., Smith, L. L., & Doyle Gentry, W. (2021, July 1). *How to identify your anger triggers.* Dummies. https://www.dummies.com/article/body-mind-spirit/emotional-health-psychology/emotional-health/anger-management/how-to-identify-your-anger-triggers-141934/

Fisher, W. (n.d.). *Empathy in marriage - 3 steps to develop it.* Dr. Wyatt Fisher. https://www.drwyattfisher.com/en-ca/blogs/marriage-blog/cultivating-more-empathy-in-marriage

Fitzgibbons, R. P. (2019, September 26). *For a healthy marriage, practice forgiveness to reduce anger.* Institute for Family Studies. https://ifstud

ies.org/blog/for-a-healthy-marriage-practice-forgiveness-to-reduce-anger

Golden, B. (2016, August 2). *How to overcome destructive anger.* Greater Good. https://greatergood.berkeley.edu/article/item/how_to_overcome_destructive_anger

Granath, J., Ingvarsson, S., von Thiele, U., & Lundberg, U. (2006). Stress management: A randomized study of cognitive behavioural therapy and yoga. *Cognitive Behaviour Therapy, 35*(1), 3–10.

Gupta, R. K., Singh, S., Bhatt, S., & Gupta, S. (2015). A Review of Mindfulness meditation and its effects on adolescents' aggression. *Online Journal of Multidisciplinary Research (OJMR), 1*(1), 12-17.

Hammond, C. (2014, July 29). *Is it bad to bottle up your anger?* BBC. https://www.bbc.com/future/article/20140729-is-it-bad-to-bottle-up-anger

Harriet Lerner quotes (author of The dance of anger). (n.d.). Goodreads. https://www.goodreads.com/author/quotes/84497.Harriet_Lerner

Hendricks, L., Bore, S., Aslinia, D., & Morriss, G. (2013). The effects of anger on the brain and body. *National forum journal of counseling and addiction, 2*(1), 2-5.

How to (really) think before you speak. (2021, April 21). Urbanyogi Live. https://urbanyogi.live/blog/how-to-really-think-before-you-speak

Lerner, J. S., & Keltner, D. (2001). Fear, anger, and risk. *Journal of Personality and Social Psychology, 81*(1), 146–159.

Lindberg, S. (2019, May 20). *Pent-up anger: Causes, symptoms, treatments, and more.* Healthline. https://www.healthline.com/health/mental-health/pent-up-anger#causes

Manning-Schaffel, V. (2017, September 16). *How being angry can (sometimes) be good for you.* NBC News; NBC News. https://www.nbcnews.com/better/health/how-being-angry-can-sometimes-be-good-you-ncna801661

Mayo Clinic. (2018). *Intermittent explosive disorder - Symptoms and causes.* Mayo Clinic. https://www.mayoclinic.org/diseases-conditions/intermittent-explosive-disorder/symptoms-causes/syc-20373921

Nunez, K. (2020, August 10). *Progressive muscle relaxation: Benefits, how-*

to, technique. Healthline. https://www.healthline.com/health/progressive-muscle-relaxation

Ohwovoriole, T. (2021, May 28). *How to manage your anger*. Verywell Mind. https://www.verywellmind.com/what-is-anger-5120208

Parrott, D. J., & Giancola, P. R. (2007). Addressing "the criterion problem" in the assessment of aggressive behavior: Development of a new taxonomic system. *Aggression and Violent Behavior, 12*(3), 280-299.

Quote by Stanley Victor Paskavich. (n.d.). Quotes Lyfe. https://www.quoteslyfe.com/quote/Always-remember-when-it-comes-to-family-161713

Quote of the week #5. (2018, October 25). The Fire to Inspire. https://thefiretoinspire.com/2018/10/25/quote-of-the-week-5/

Rothenberg, A. (1971). On anger. *American Journal of Psychiatry, 128*(4), 454-460.

Rose, W. G. (2021, November 11). *The dangers of bottling up our emotions*. Verywell Mind. https://www.verywellmind.com/the-dangers-of-bottling-up-our-emotions-5207825

Schieman, S. (2006). Anger. In Turner, J. H. (Ed.). *Handbook of the sociology of emotions* (pp. 493-515). Springer.

Schwartz, A. N. (n.d.). *Anger and why it's a problem*. https://www.mentalhelp.net/anger/why-its-a-problem/

Scott, E. (2021, March 19). *Simple ways to get anger and stress under control*. Verywell Mind. https://www.verywellmind.com/how-anger-problems-can-affect-your-health-3145075

Seladi-Schulman, J. (2018, July 23). *What part of the brain controls emotions?* Health Line. https://www.healthline.com/health/what-part-of-the-brain-controls-emotions#anger

Spiritual quotation by Thich Nhat Hanh. (n.d.). Spirituality & Practice. https://www.spiritualityandpractice.com/quotes/quotations/view/13940/spiritual-quotation

Thomas Jefferson quotes. (n.d.). BrainyQuote. https://www.brainyquote.com/quotes/thomas_jefferson_132201

Staicu, M.-L., & Cuţov, M. (2010). Anger and health risk behaviors.

Journal of Medicine and Life, 3(4), 372–375. https://www.ncbi.nlm.nih.gov/pmc/articles/PMC3019061/

Stevens, T. G. (2010). *You can choose to be happy: "rise above" anxiety, anger, and depression, with research evidence* (2nd ed.). Wheeler-Sutton Pub. Co.

Strong, D. (2015, May 29). *7 ways anger is ruining your health.* Everyday Health. https://www.everydayhealth.com/news/ways-anger-ruining-your-health/

Sukhodolsky, D. G., Smith, S. D., McCauley, S. A., Ibrahim, K., & Piasecka, J. B. (2016). Behavioral interventions for anger, irritability, and aggression in children and adolescents. *Journal of Child and Adolescent Psychopharmacology, 26*(1), 58–64.

IMAGE REFERENCES

Cowley, Nathan. (2018, March 1). *Man in a blue and brown plaid dress shirt touching his hair.* Pexels. [Image]. https://www.pexels.com/photo/man-in-blue-and-brown-plaid-dress-shirt-touching-his-hair-897817/

Garrison, David. (2019, April 17). *Woman holding her head.* Pexels. [Image]. https://www.pexels.com/photo/woman-holding-her-head-2128817/

Grabowska, Karolina. (2020, June 25). *Peaceful lady sitting in Padmasana poses while meditating on a mat.* Pexels. [Image]. https://www.pexels.com/photo/peaceful-lady-sitting-in-padmasana-pose-while-meditating-on-mat-4498220/

Hiett, Elijah. (2017, August 9). *Alone on a mountain.* Unsplash. [Image]. https://unsplash.com/photos/wW0BUXTTUmU

Krukov, Yan. (2021, April 25). *A woman standing in front of the group.* Pexels. [Image]. https://www.pexels.com/photo/a-woman-standing-in-front-of-the-group-7640822/

Minda, Ankush. (2018, February 5). *Away we go..up in the sky.* Unsplash. [Image]. https://unsplash.com/photos/4Xy08NbMBLM

Miroshnichenko, Tima. (2020, October 31). *A woman in a black tank top and black shorts.* Pexels. [Image]. https://www.pexels.com/photo/a-woman-in-black-tank-top-and-black-shorts-5750636/

Nilov, Mikhail. (2021, May 17). *Sad boy in a gray sweater sitting on the floor.* Pexels. [Image]. https://www.pexels.com/photo/sad-boy-in-gray-sweater-sitting-on-the-floor-7929419/

Piacquadio, Andrea. (2018, September 8). *Mad formal executive man yelling at the camera.* Pexels. [Image]. https://www.pexels.com/photo/mad-formal-executive-man-yelling-at-camera-3760790/

Piacquadio, Andrea. (2020, April 4). *Woman in gray tank top.* Pexels. [Image]. https://www.pexels.com/photo/woman-in-gray-tank-top-3812746/

Pinisetti, Ravi. (2017, July 11). *Calm landscape.* Unsplash. [Image]. https://unsplash.com/photos/1zikZJVXSfA

Pixabay. (2016, December 31). *Human fist.* Pexels. [Image]. https://www.pexels.com/photo/human-fist-163431/

Plenio, Johannes. (2018, August 16). *Star reflection.* Unsplash. [Image]. https://unsplash.com/photos/DKix6Un55mw

RODNAE Productions. (2021, June 25). *A girl looking at the window.* Pexels. [Image]. https://www.pexels.com/photo/a-girl-looking-at-the-window-8489064/

RODNAE Productions. (2021, November 27). *Parents arguing in front of a child.* Pexels. [Image]. https://www.pexels.com/photo/parents-arguing-in-front-of-a-child-6003561/

Rychvalsky, Lukas. (2017, November 5). *Lonely.* Unsplash. [Image]. https://unsplash.com/photos/o0GhPKxe5GM

Samkov, Ivan. (2021, January 30). *A man and a woman doing yoga.* Pexels. [Image]. https://www.pexels.com/photo/a-man-and-a-woman-doing-yoga-6648543/

Summer, Liza. (2021, January 3). *Sad multiracial women hugging at home.* Pexels. [Image]. https://www.pexels.com/search/anger%20expressions/

Visalli, Antonio. (2018, December 18). *Man wearing a black shirt.* Unsplash. [Image]. https://unsplash.com/photos/ap3_MjQ1DLk

Weber, Timur. (2021, June 22). *A couple talking while arguing.* Pexels. [Image]. https://www.pexels.com/photo/a-couple-talking-while-arguing-8560383/